P9-DFL-713

THE
BIRDER'S
COMPANION

STEPHEN MOSS

ILLUSTRATIONS BY CLIVE DOBSON

FIREFLY BOOKS

For my wonderful children: David, James, Charlie, George and Daisy.

A FIREFLY BOOK

Published by Firefly Books Ltd. 2007

Text copyright © 2007 Stephen Moss
Illustrations copyright © 2007 Clive Dobson

All rights reserved. No part of this publication may be reproduced, stored in a retrieval system, or transmitted in any form or by any means, electronic, mechanical, photocopying, recording or otherwise, without the prior written permission of the Publisher.

First printing

Publisher Cataloging-in-Publication Data (U.S.)
Moss, Stephen.
 Birder's companion / Stephen Moss.
 [192] p. : ill. ; cm.
 Includes bibliographical references and index.
 Features sections on avian physiology, evolution and classification, population, distribution, feeding, breeding and migration.
 ISBN-13: 978-1-55407-212-5 (pbk.)
 ISBN-10: 1-55407-212-3 (pbk.)
 1. Birds. 2. Bird watching. I. Title.
 598/.07234 dc22   QL677.5.M677 2007

Library and Archives Canada Cataloguing in Publication
Moss, Stephen, 1960–
 Birder's companion / Stephen Moss.
 Includes bibliographical references and index.
 ISBN-13: 978-1-55407-212-5
 ISBN-10: 1-55407-212-3
 1. Bird watching. I. Title.
 QL677.5.M68 2007   598.072'34   C2006-906631-0

Published in the United States by
Firefly Books (U.S.) Inc.
P.O. Box 1338, Ellicott Station
Buffalo, New York 14205

Published in Canada by
Firefly Books Ltd.
66 Leek Crescent
Richmond Hill, Ontario L4B 1H1

Front cover and interior illustrations: Clive Dobson

Printed in Canada

CONTENTS

ACKNOWLEDGMENTS

I have many people to thank for the genesis, production and completion of this book. First and foremost, my wife Suzanne, who was her usual tower of strength and support during its writing, despite giving birth to her own three productions during that time. I persuaded several people to read all or part of the text to root out any errors, misconceptions and lack of clarity. Of these, Chris Harbard brought his vast experience to the job, aided and abetted by Chris Watson and Daniel Orsorio. In quiet moments on a filming trip to Patagonia, my colleagues John Atchison and Mike Dilger also made many helpful suggestions.

But my greatest gratitude must go to Mike Unwin, who took my original text and edited it to within an inch of its life, adding clarity, structure and humor. Working with him has been an unalloyed pleasure, and I hope to do so again in the very near future.

INTRODUCTION

I have spent much of my life fielding questions about birds from people I encounter in various places. Not surprisingly then, I yearned for an easy reference source that provided all the answers in a single place, something like a walking encyclopedia on birds, a resource that is informative and accurate but also accessible and straightforward. My hope for this book is that it offers the reader a similarly friendly approach to learning about birds. I also want it to be relevant to readers having a wide range of interest in birds, from the keen birder who heads out every weekend, rain or shine, to the self-styled naturalist who is simply curious about the world.

Questions are a natural way of focusing our interest. The simple question-and-answer format used here takes you straight to the answer without swamping you in information you may not want or need. Instead of producing a dense textbook on the almost infinitely complex lives of birds, I have presented the information in easily digestible, bite-sized chunks that you can consume at leisure.

I began the writing process by collecting and compiling raw questions from a broad spectrum of people, including friends and family, beginners and experts. Some questions were fascinating, some ludicrous and some unanswerable, but all played a part in revealing the kind of things people want to know about birds. If you were part of this process, I hope you find your answer here, and with luck, a lot more besides.

From the myriad of questions about birds, I chose more than 500, and arranged them in ten chapters, each tackling a major theme, such as feeding, breeding or migration. This format makes it easy for the reader to choose how to read the book. You can start at the beginning and read straight through, or you can follow your curiosity and browse and hop among the various sections. The comprehensive index helps you locate any question you want answered plus some you never thought of asking. From there I hope you will be drawn further into the book, where you will find equally interesting answers to related questions or gain a deeper insight into a particular subject.

You will find the text is liberally sprinkled with headlined boxes containing nuggets of information. These are what I call record breakers and they list superlatives such as the biggest, smallest, highest, fastest and so on. Being records, they are subject to certain qualifications: some, such as those concerned with longevity, may have already been surpassed by the time the book hits the shelves; others have their absolute accuracy open to question. And all of course are subject in the first place to the advent and accuracy of record keeping and simply reflect what has been measured or studied to date, which means they are not the final word on the subject. Facts and statistics, especially those related to the latest scientific discoveries, often show a distinct bias toward European or North American species, only because that is where most research takes place. All facts published here were checked against at least two further sources, and usually more. I used a number of reference books for this process and the most important of these are listed in the bibliography. Where there is any measure of doubt, I couched the information in suitably non-committal terms, such as "probably," "it is claimed," etc. If you discover a newer or more accurate record, please let me know (via the publishers) and I'll be happy to include it in future editions.

So who exactly is this book for? My longtime friend and birding companion Daniel Osorio gave me a typically backhanded compliment when he said it would appeal to intelligent, inquiring eleven-year-old boys — the same age he and I were when we first met. While that may be true, I hope that it will appeal also to eleven-year-old girls, since there are far too few women birders. That it might spark an interest would help to redress the balance. Ultimately, however, I would like to think that this book has something to offer readers of all ages, and that it is equally suitable for experienced birders, complete novices and anyone in between. Wherever you may be in that continuum, I hope you enjoy reading it. I hope also that you are motivated to go outside and look anew at birds — which to my mind are the most elegant, fascinating and delightful of all God's creatures.

Stephen Moss
December 2006

1 WHAT IS A BIRD?

PHYSIOLOGY

ANATOMY

What is a bird?

A bird is a warm-blooded, egg-laying vertebrate (animal with a backbone). It has a body covered with feathers and forelimbs modified to form wings. Technically speaking, birds are all members of the class Aves.

What makes birds unique?

In a word: feathers. This is the only characteristic unique to birds, as opposed to mammals (which are also warm-blooded), some reptiles and three strange mammals (which also lay eggs) and bats (which can also fly). No other creature has evolved feathers, but all birds — even flightless ones such as penguins — have them.

Are birds warm-blooded?

Yes, just like mammals, birds are warm-blooded, or "homoeothermic." This means they can (and must) maintain a constant body temperature of between 100 and 109 degrees Fahrenheit (38–43°C), regardless of the temperature outside.

In cold weather, birds help retain this heat by fluffing out their feathers to trap an insulating layer of warm air close to their body.

Some species also huddle together in communal roosts to avoid losing heat. Birds that give birth to naked young ("altricial" or "nidicolous" species) have to brood their chicks, which remain cold-blooded ("poikilothermic") until they fledge. The adults do so by covering the chicks with a naked brood patch on their underparts so that their body heat keeps the youngsters warm.

Do birds have a skeleton?

Like all vertebrates, birds have an internal skeleton, but it has been cunningly customized to suit a bird's unique requirements. Many of the bones are hollow and criss-crossed with internal struts, making them strong yet incredibly light. This keeps a bird's body weight to a minimum, allowing it to take to the air and fly. A bird's skeleton also has two important modifications: the hind limbs and pelvis have shifted to enable it to walk or hop on two legs, while the forelimbs have been modified into wings, enabling most birds to fly.

The huge, keeled breastbone (take a close look at a roast chicken!) is also a special flight adaptation, since it holds the powerful muscles required for flapping the wings.

How do birds breathe?

Like mammals, birds have lungs, which extract oxygen from the air, pump it around the body via the blood and expel waste carbon dioxide. Unlike mammals, birds also have a secondary system of air sacs located around their body and even inside their bones. This unique adaptation enables birds to circulate oxygen much more efficiently — vital for allowing them to fly without getting out of breath!

Big bird

The world's largest living bird is the ostrich, which can weigh up to 300 pounds (136 kg) — about 85,000 times as heavy as the world's smallest species (see page 30). One specimen was said to have reached 330 pounds (150 kg). Unsurprisingly, the ostrich is also the world's tallest living bird, occasionally reaching a height of over 8 feet (2.44 m).

How fast does a bird's heart beat?

This depends on the bird's size and what it is doing. Large birds tend to have slow heart rates (that of the ostrich is only about 38 beats per minute), while the heartbeat of most songbirds ranges between 200 and 500 beats per minute. Hummingbirds may even reach a heart rate of more than 1,000 beats per minute. Heart rates increase in cold weather and when a bird is under stress. Our own resting heart rate averages about 72 beats per minute.

Do birds perspire?

No. Birds don't have any sweat glands on their skin, so they lose excess heat by panting and seeking shade.

Do birds have teeth?

No modern bird has true teeth — these were jettisoned during the evolutionary drive to get light enough for flight. But some species have sharp cutting edges on their bill. A few tropical species such as the African barbets and the unique tooth-billed pigeon of Samoa have toothlike notches on their mandibles, but these are not used for chewing food. Inside a bird's egg the developing chick has an "egg tooth" with which it chips its way out. This is not a true tooth, however, and it drops off a few days after birth.

What is the difference between a "bill" and a "beak"?

Except for spelling, nothing at all: the two terms are interchangeable (though birders and ornithologists tend to prefer the term "bill"). Both refer to the horny projection at the front of every bird's skull, consisting of the upper and lower mandibles — essentially the equivalent of a mammal's jaws.

What is a bird's bill made from?

Like feathers, it is made from keratin, a light, strong and very flexible form of protein. This extraordinary substance can take many forms, enabling bills to tackle all kind of jobs.

What do birds use their bills for?

Apart from actually feeding, birds use their bills for catching food (herons and insect-eating songbirds), carrying and storing food (pelicans and puffins), digging or drilling nest holes (woodpeckers) and preening (all birds). Because their forelimbs have adapted into wings, birds must do with their bills the tasks we humans perform with our hands and fingers. Some birds, such as certain storks and albatrosses, also clatter with their bills as part of their courtship display.

Why do some birds have such strangely shaped bills?

Settling the bills

The longest bill belongs to the Australian white pelican, and may reach a length of 19 inches (48 cm). The shortest bill belongs to the glossy swiftlet of Southeast Asia, at just 0.16 inch (0.41 cm) long. The longest bill relative to body size belongs to the sword-billed hummingbird of the northern Andes and measures 3.5 to 4.3 inches (8.89–10.92 cm), more than half the bird's total length. This extraordinary appendage enables the bird to reach nectar hidden deep inside long flowers such as the climbing passionflower. The bill is so heavy that, when perched, the bird has to hold it at an angle to avoid toppling over!

Every bill has evolved to suit a particular feeding technique, and this has produced some weird shapes. Among the strangest is that of puffins, whose bill has an "elasticated" base so that they can hold several small fish at once; spoonbills, whose spatulate bill contains sensitive nerve endings that detect minute food items; skimmers, whose lower mandible is longer than the upper one, enabling them to "skim" the surface of the water for morsels of food; and crossbills, whose upper and lower mandibles are crossed to allow them to pry the seeds out of pinecones. But perhaps the weirdest bill of all is that of a shorebird found in New Zealand, aptly named the wrybill. This is the only bird in the world whose bill curves sideways, enabling it to probe for insect food under rocks and stones.

Why do some birds have deformed bills?

The keratin of a bird's bill grows continually to compensate for being worn down by use. But if the tip breaks from the upper mandible, the tip of the lower one will have nothing to wear against and so will grow abnormally long. If a beak becomes twisted to the side, both mandibles can grow but will cross over. Birds with deformed beaks can survive only as long as they are able to feed.

Do birds have tongues?

Yes, they all do, though this organ is more important for some birds than for others. Most birds do not have much of a sense of taste (see page 25), so many groups, including storks and pelicans, have very small tongues. Parrots, by contrast, have a large, fleshy tongue used for manipulating their food; hummingbirds have a long, thin one to poke into flowers for nectar; and flamingos have a whopper, which helps to pump out water while they are filter feeding. Woodpeckers have proportionally the longest tongue of all; it is rooted at the back of the skull, and its barbed, sticky tip is designed for extracting insects from under loose bark.

What do birds use their feet for?

As well as the obvious functions of walking, running, hopping and swimming (see Chapter 5), birds use their feet for a number of other

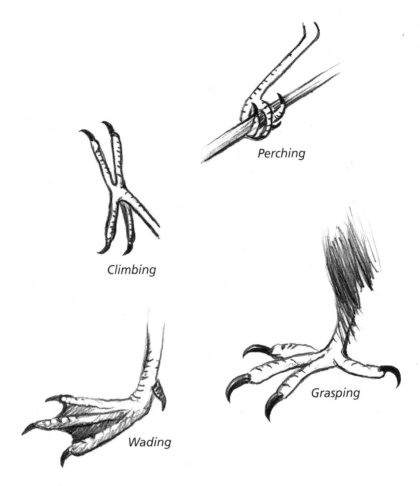

Perching

Climbing

Grasping

Wading

The foot structure of every bird serves a specific purpose, such as perching, climbing, wading or grasping prey. Form matches function.

purposes. These include perching (all passerines and many other birds), catching food (especially birds of prey and owls), climbing (woodpeckers, creepers and nuthatches) and digging (underground-dwelling species such as the burrowing owl). Some species, including various wild game birds and the domestic chicken, even use their feet in combat with rival males — hence the sport of cockfighting.

How many toes do birds have?

Most birds have four toes on each foot. Some have only three, and the ostrich has just two. Birds' toes are arranged in one of various configurations: all four pointing forward for gripping onto vertical surfaces (e.g., swifts), three toes pointing forward and one back for perching (passerines) or two toes forward and two back for climbing or grasping objects (woodpeckers, cuckoos and parrots). One species, the osprey, can even adjust the arrangement: normally it points three toes forward and one back, but when catching fish it points two forward and two back to get a better grip on its slippery prey.

What are webbed feet for?

Many unrelated families, including wildfowl (ducks, geese and swans), gulls, cormorants and petrels, have fully webbed feet, which enable them to swim more effectively. Other waterbirds, such as grebes and coots, have developed lobed (partially webbed) feet for the same reason. Webbing is not the only way that feet have adapted to help a bird get around: birds that habitually walk on aquatic vegetation, such as rails and jacanas, have elongated toes to spread their weight across the surface; some birds that live in cold climates, such as ptarmigan, have feathered feet that act as snowshoes.

Tongue-tied

The bird with the longest tongue relative to body size is the wryneck, whose tongue may measure more than 3 inches (7.62 cm) — about half its body length.

Do birds have knees?

Yes, but not where some people think they are! A bird's knee is actually concealed in the plumage at the top of its leg, whereas the joint that is often assumed to be the knee (roughly halfway up the visible leg) is in fact the anklebone. This has led to the popular misconception that birds' knees bend backward!

PLUMAGE

Why do birds have feathers?

Feathers do two main jobs for birds: they allow them to fly and they keep them warm. Fossil evidence suggests that feathers probably evolved from reptilian scales to keep ancestral birds warm in cold climates. Flight would thus have been an evolutionary afterthought.

What advantages do feathers bring?

Feathers are miraculously versatile things. Their strength and lightness allow a bird to get airborne without using up too much energy, while their streamlined shape reduces air resistance. They also enable birds to maintain a constant body temperature by dispersing heat in hot weather and trapping heat when it gets chillier. Last, but certainly not least, feathers are vital for courtship displays, in which one (usually male) bird flaunts his fancy plumage to attract a mate or repel a rival.

What are feathers made from?

Feathers are made from a horny substance called keratin, which is also found in a bird's beak and claws — and indeed in human hair and fingernails. Feathers have several component parts: the central shaft, which is hollow at the base and attaches to the bird's skin; the barbs, or side branches, which are attached to the shaft; and tiny barbules, which branch off the barbs and mesh with each other, giving the feather its unique combination of strength and lightness. Different types of feathers have different uses: for example, the large wing feathers enable a bird to fly, the "contour" feathers cover and streamline its body and the soft downy ones keep it warm.

How many feathers does a bird have?

This varies enormously, from fewer than 1,000 for some species of hummingbird to more than 25,000 in the case of the whistling swan of North America (most of its feathers are on its head and neck). The number of feathers tends to increase with the size of the bird. Most passerines have between 3,000 and 5,000 feathers, while a bald eagle has more than 7,000. Waterbirds tend to have more feathers than landbirds to help keep them warm and dry.

What are "primaries," "secondaries" and "tertials"?

These are all types of feathers found in the wing. Primaries are the longest feathers at the end, secondaries are the shorter ones along the

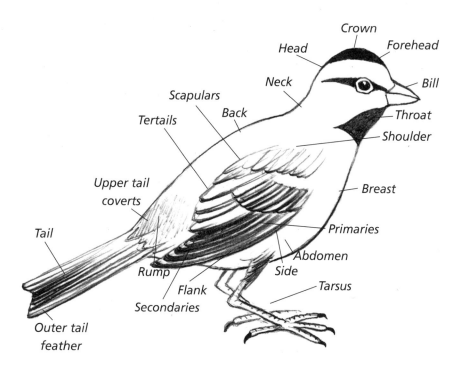

Learning the terminology for the bare and feathered parts of birds aids in identifying them. Top-flight birders are experts in bird topography.

inner part of the wing and tertials are the ones close to the bird's body. Other wing feathers include scapulars and wing coverts.

What is "bird topography"?

This technical term refers to the way we define and name the various external features of a bird's plumage (along with its bare parts, such as the bill and legs). Although birds may be very different in shape and appearance, the feathers of all birds are arranged in the same basic way. Knowing bird topography helps you describe a bird's appearance and is vital for understanding molt (see page 20). It also helps birders identify similar-looking species by noting subtle differences in their plumage features.

Legging it

The ostrich has the longest legs of any bird, reaching a whopping 4 feet (1.22 m) from hip to toe. The longest legs relative to body size belong to the black-winged stilt (and its various relatives) and constitute about 60 percent of its total length.

How does a bird look after its feathers?

Feather care is a top priority for birds. Techniques include preening (using the bill to clean individual feathers), scratching (with its feet), bathing (either in water or dust) and oiling (secreting a waterproof substance to avoid becoming waterlogged). Many birds have a special preen gland just above the base of their tail. This gland secretes oil, which birds spread across the surface of their feathers with their bill.

What happens if a bird damages its feathers?

Birds lead a strenuous life, and feathers take a constant battering; they are often lost or broken and may become covered with a harmful substance such as oil. Generally, new feathers replace broken or lost ones when a bird molts (see page 21). As long as a bird can still feed and fly, it will probably survive, though it may be unable to migrate or get away from predators. If oil covers the plumage of a bird, however, it may lose its ability to fly or swim and will be unable to maintain the correct body temperature. Unless it gets clean quickly, the bird will almost certainly die.

How do birds bathe?

Usually, like us, in water. The favorite bathing method of most birds is to partially submerge themselves (either at the edge of a pond or in a puddle or birdbath) and splash liquid over their wings and body while frantically shaking to make sure all the feathers get wet. Many waterbirds, such as gulls and ducks, bathe while sitting on the surface of the water; some seabirds, though, such as terns and frigatebirds, are reluctant to do so for fear of becoming waterlogged. Instead, they plunge down onto the surface of the sea from above, briefly wetting their plumage as they do so. A few species, such as parrots and wood-peckers, deliberately expose themselves to rainfall, while others, including hornbills, rub themselves against wet tropical vegetation.

What about "dust-bathing"?

Dust-bathing, or "dusting," is a specialized form of behavior in which a bird wriggles in dust or sand, tosses the fine particles over its wings and body, rubs the dust into its plumage and then shakes it out again. This removes excess preen oil from the feathers and keeps them free of grease. Dust-bathing also helps rid the feathers and skin of harmful parasites such as lice and mites. Many species use dusting to keep their plumage in tip-top condition. These include ostriches, rheas, gamebirds, bustards, sandgrouse, hoopoes and rollers. Fewer passerines do so, but among them are larks, wrens and the house sparrow.

What are the other advantages of a well-kept plumage?

A bird's general health owes much to the quality of its plumage, as feathers are vital for many basic life functions such as flight and heat regulation. Male birds with the glossiest, brightest plumage also tend to attract the "best" females, as a healthy plumage is a sign of the bird's ability to reproduce and have lots of healthy offspring.

Is the plumage of waterbirds waterproof?

In many species, yes. And water does not flow only off a duck's back, but also off the backs of grebes, coots, auks, geese and swans. These birds regularly anoint their plumage with oil from their preen gland, enabling them to spend long periods on the surface of the water. Several families that spend much of their time at sea or swimming, however, cannot fully waterproof their plumage. These include frigatebirds, which are in the air whenever they are away from their nest, and cormorants, which are obliged to stretch out their wings after feeding to dry them.

Do birds carry parasites?

Many birds are crawling with unwanted passengers such as mites, ticks, feather lice and louse flies — parasites that feed on the blood, feathers or shed skin of their host. These pests generally latch on to a bird while it is still in the nest and remain on it for the rest of its life. Generally, parasites do little harm unless the bird becomes sick, in which case they may become too numerous for the bird to cope. Healthy birds keep their parasites in check by regular preening, bathing and dust-bathing. Some, like the jay, may also engage in "anting," the practice of picking up ants and rubbing them into the plumage, or simply allowing ants to swarm all over the body. The formic acid the ants secrete kills many parasites.

COLOR

How do birds get their colors?

Pigments produce some colors present in feathers; the refraction of light within the feather structure produces other colors, such as the iridescent blues, greens and purples of hummingbirds. Our perception of a bird's color is also affected by the quality of light: sunrise and sunset

Tails of the unexpected

The bird with the longest tail feathers is the male crested argus pheasant of Southeast Asia. These may reach a length of 68 inches (173 cm) — almost three-quarters of the bird's total length. The length of the tail feathers increases yearly, with the oldest birds generally having the longest tails. The longest tail feathers ever recorded, however, belonged to an ornamental chicken bred in Japan and were reputed to have reached an amazing 34 feet (10.36 m).

The longest tail relative to body size belongs to the male ribbon-tailed astrapia, a bird-of-paradise found in New Guinea, which has a tail 35 inches (89 cm) long — three-quarters of the bird's total length. In Europe and North America, the barn swallow's tail can grow to almost 5 inches (12.7 cm) long — two-thirds of the bird's total length.

make colors appear richer and warmer, while harsh midday sun may "burn out" a bird's plumage, making it appear paler than usual. Some birds obtain their color from the food they eat: a diet of shrimps colors the flamingo.

Why do different birds have different colors?

Color in plumage has several different purposes. Many birds have a dull, brownish plumage to camouflage themselves for protection against predators; others sport a bright, garish plumage to attract a mate. Sometimes the two can be seen in the same species: the bright colors of a male mallard contrast dramatically with the subtle brown tones of his mate, who can remain undetected while sitting on her eggs.

How do birds use colors to camouflage themselves?

Some birds have a "cryptic" pattern, so they can blend in with their chosen background — as in a nightjar sitting on a branch or a bittern freezing among the reeds. But many colorful tropical birds, such as tanagers and parakeets, can also be surprisingly hard to pick out against the pale green foliage of the treetops. The bold colors and patterns of these birds serve to "disrupt" their outline, making them harder to see. Some birds that spend part of their life in snow adopt an all-white plumage in winter: the rock ptarmigan has three different seasonal plumages, each of which enables it to camouflage itself as the landscape changes around it.

Why do so many birds have dark wingtips?

Because melanin, the pigment that makes feathers dark, also makes them stronger. Having stronger feathers at the tips of wings where they are more likely to become worn is an advantage for birds.

Why do some birds have bright flashes of color?

Many birds, especially small passerines such as wood-warblers, have striking white or yellow patches on their wings, tail or rump. These patches confuse a predator by distracting it when the bird takes flight, and also alert the rest of the flock to danger by acting as warning signals when flashed in flight. Often these markings are covered up when the bird is perched, so it can stay hidden from view until it takes off. Bright colors are also evident in breeding displays.

What are "albino," "melanistic" and "leucistic" plumages?

These are all abnormal plumage types, caused either by too little or too much of a particular pigment in the feathers. A lack of all pigments causes albinism, making the whole or part of the bird's plumage appear white. Melanism is the result of too much of the dark pigment melanin and makes the bird look darker than usual. Leucism, a much rarer condition, is the result of reduced amounts of pigment in the plumage, giving the bird a "washed out" appearance. Even rarer, "xanthochroism" refers to an abnormally yellow plumage and is most often seen in cage birds such as parrots whose diet is lacking in the correct minerals. Albinism occurs more frequently in certain groups than others, being commonest in wildfowl, crows and thrushes.

What is a "phase"?

A phase (also sometimes called a "morph") refers to the presence in a wild bird population of two or more distinctive plumage forms, which may occur in birds that freely interbreed with each other. Examples include the pale phase and dark phase of the parasitic jaeger, the red and grey forms of the screech owl and the "bridled" form of the common murre. A single genetic difference is thought to cause these forms, rather like eye color in humans, and they do not mean that the individuals involved belong to different subspecies, even though they may look very different. Species with two different morphs are known as "dimorphic," while those, such as male ruffs, that have many different color forms are known as "polymorphic." Morphs are most widely found in two groups, owls and nightjars, in which up to one-third of all species may show distinct plumage phases.

What is "sexual dimorphism"?

Simply put, this is the difference between the male and female of the same species, which may be expressed in size, color, plumage features or a combination of all three.

MOLT

Why do birds molt?

Because if they didn't, their plumage would get so worn and tattered they would have trouble finding food, coping with the elements, breeding and, ultimately, surviving. Broken feathers and worn plumage hamper flight in particular. Birds also molt to adopt a more showy plumage for courtship and breeding. This may simply be a brighter version of their usual plumage or, in some cases — for example, in many shorebirds, grebes, loons and auks — a completely different-looking plumage just for the breeding season. Extreme examples include the African widowbirds and whydahs, whose males exhibit

Male

Female

In some species of birds, such as the black oystercatcher and the blue jay, the male and female are identical. In sexually dimorphic species, the sexes differ in various ways. Most often the male of such a species is more colorful than the female, as in the case of the mallard.

exotic breeding plumes with incredibly long tails, yet outside the breeding season become a nondescript streaky-brown, with short tails.

How do birds molt?

A new feather, growing from a follicle in the skin, gradually pushes out the old one. Molting usually follows a regular sequence within each feather group. So a passerine such as a thrush or warbler

Ground shakers

The largest bird that ever lived was probably aepyornis, or the elephant bird of Madagascar. Its weight has been estimated as about 990 pounds (449 kg) — more than three times as heavy as an ostrich. It probably survived as late as the 17th century. The giant moa of New Zealand, which became extinct at about the same time, was taller, standing over 11 feet (3.35 m) but weighed a mere 530 pounds (240 kg).

usually molts its flight feathers from the innermost (and shortest) primary feather outward, toward the longest feathers on the outside edge of the wing. Birds of prey have a more complex molt pattern, the process beginning with one of the middle primary feathers on the wing and progressing in both directions from them. Many waterbirds, such as ducks, geese and swans, shed all their flight feathers at the same time and are often unable to fly for several weeks until the new feathers have grown.

How often do birds molt?

All adult birds molt at least once a year, and many species — including some waders, gulls and terns — do so twice, adopting a different appearance during the breeding season. Birds molt more frequently in their first year, sometimes shedding their feathers up to three times (from down to juvenal plumage, juvenal to "first winter" plumage and finally to full adult breeding plumage the spring after they are born).

How long does molt take?

For most birds, molt takes a month or two, though for some passerines such as the white wagtail it can take up to 75 days. Long-distance migrants such as wood-warblers and flycatchers, which need to grow new flight feathers in plenty of time to make the journey south after breeding, tend to molt more quickly than sedentary species.

Do all birds molt at the same time of year?

Not exactly, but the majority do so soon after the end of the breeding season. Molting makes a bird more vulnerable to attack by predators and may also make it less able (in some cases, completely unable) to fly. Most birds molt at a time of year when food is plentiful, foliage in which to hide is dense and no valuable energy need be used in courtship or migration. Most migratory birds molt before they head off, taking advantage of new flight feathers for the journey. A few (such as swallows and some birds of prey), however, wait until after they reach their destination to molt.

Air movers

The largest North American bird is the trumpeter swan, which weighs up to 28 pounds (12.7 kg), while the tallest North American bird is the whooping crane, at 5 feet (1.52 m).

What is "eclipse" plumage?

Eclipse plumage is simply a temporary plumage that several families of birds, notably ducks, adopt: the male molts all his colorful feathers after courtship and mating and resembles the duller female for several months.

What are "worn" and "fresh" plumages?

These terms describe different stages in the molt cycle. "Worn" usually applies to an adult bird toward the end of the breeding season, when the toll of finding food for hungry young has left its plumage looking very tattered. In contrast, once it has molted, an adult acquires "fresh" plumage, as does a juvenal following the shedding of its original downy feathers.

What are "breeding" and "nonbreeding" plumages?

These are the very different plumages some bird species adopt during and outside the breeding season. Because birds molt at different times of year, however, a bird may have adopted "breeding" plumage well before courtship actually starts, or may acquire its "nonbreeding" plumage while still feeding young. To make things even more confusing, many otherwise reputable field guides persist in using the even less accurate terms "summer" and "winter" plumages — despite the fact that some dark-headed gulls may molt into their "summer" plumage as early as January! To resolve the confusion, some ornithologists have proposed a new terminology, using the term "basic" to replace "nonbreeding" or "winter" plumage, and "alternate" to replace "breeding" or "summer" plumage.

What is the difference between "immature" and "juvenal" plumages?

"Juvenal" plumage is specifically defined as the first "proper" plumage acquired at fledging, that is, after the bird sheds its original downy feathers. "Immature" is a less well-defined term and simply means any plumage between juvenal and full adult — which, in the case of larger birds such as eagles and gulls, may cover half a dozen distinct plumages spanning a period of several years.

King of the wingers

The title of the world's largest flying bird is shared by the Andean condor, weighing up to 33 pounds (14.97 kg); the great bustard, males of which weigh an average of 37 pounds (16.78 kg); and the African kori bustard, which may occasionally reach a weight of around 40 pounds (18.14 kg).

SENSES

Which is the most important sense for birds?

In all but a very few cases, their sight. Birds tend to have proportionately larger eyes and more acute vision than other vertebrates, and most bird species depend on it to find food or avoid predators. Hearing is also important, especially for songbirds and nocturnal species such as owls and nightjars. Some birds, including seabirds, scavengers and nocturnal hunters, also have a powerful sense of smell.

Which is birds' least important sense?

Their taste. Most birds have only between 30 and 70 taste buds, whereas humans have about 9,000! Some notable exceptions are domestic chickens, which have about 250 to 350 taste buds, and parrots, which have up to 400 on their large, fleshy tongues. Birds generally do not distinguish between bitter and sweet tastes, though they can detect salt, which is an important dietary supplement for many species. Their lack of a refined ability to taste is probably because most birds swallow their food very rapidly, without chewing it as we do.

How well do birds see?

Birds' eyes, like those of other vertebrates, are complex organs, able to process visual information and send signals to the brain that allow the bird to interpret the world around it. Without sight, birds would find it almost impossible to fly around without bumping into things, let alone find food or dodge predators. It is generally assumed that birds see better than we do, and it is true that groups such as diurnal birds of prey have much better eyesight than humans. "Better" means that they have a greater ability to discern distant objects, probably somewhere between two and five times the power of human eyes.

Do birds have binocular vision?

Most do not. Virtually all birds have eyes on either side of their head. This gives them a greater field of view than ours but means that they lack the combined focus of two eyes (binocular vision) that enables us to judge perspective and distance. Having a greater field of view helps birds find food and avoid predators; indeed some, such as woodcocks and sandgrouse, have eyes that protrude from their sockets so they can see more or less all around them. The only birds that do have binocular vision are hunters such as hawks, eagles and owls. Having both eyes facing forward gives them a major advantage when hunting down their victim, though of course it considerably reduces their field of view.

Can any birds turn their heads through 360 degrees?

Not quite. But owls can turn their heads through an arc of 270 degrees, using specially adapted bones in their neck. This is because, unlike other birds, owls are unable to turn their eyes in their sockets. Many birds are able to see through an arc of up to 320 degrees, however, by a combination of turning their head and changing the position of their eyes. The wryneck is another species that can turn its head through almost 360 degrees.

Can birds see colors?

Most birds probably see color better than we do, perceiving richer tones and some wavelengths of light that we cannot, such as the ultraviolet end of the spectrum. This helps them spot items of food and also explains the prominence of color in plumage and courtship displays. Many nocturnal birds have poor color vision, though, as this improves their sensitivity to low light levels. Penguins, too, have worse color vision than other birds, probably because the environment in which penguins live is mainly monochromatic!

Can birds see in the dark?

Yes, up to a point. No birds can see in total darkness, but many have much better night vision than we do, including the ability to see in very low light levels. Several groups of birds, such as owls and nightjars, are predominantly nocturnal. Others, including tidal feeders such as waterfowl and shorebirds, are often active after dark. The majority of migratory birds prefer to travel by night.

How do owls find their prey?

By using a combination of good night vision, the ability to perceive tiny sounds moving creatures make and the kind of predictive ability that allows a car driver to travel a familiar route after dark. Some, such as the barn owl, hunt over open spaces where there are few obstacles. Others, like the eastern screech owl, have small home territories where they remain all year, allowing them to use their detailed knowledge of the terrain to hunt, even when they cannot see perfectly.

Which birds have the best eyesight?

It is often said that birds of prey such as the peregrine have eyesight that matches the power of binoculars — that is, 8 or 10 times as good as human sight. This is probably an exaggeration, though undoubtedly their vision is considerably better than ours and probably the best of any living creature's.

Do birds have ears?

Yes, though they are normally hard to see, as they are simply sockets in the side of the head, rather than the protuberances that humans and other mammals display. Incidentally, the ear tufts on species such as the long-eared owl are not for hearing at all and may have evolved for camouflage.

How well do birds hear?

Whopping wings

The greatest wingspan probably belongs to the wandering albatross, with a recorded length of almost 12 feet (3.66 m), though some individuals of this species and the royal albatross may have even longer wings! For total wing area, the title goes to the Andean condor, whose wingspan reaches almost 10 feet (3 m). But today's giants are dwarfed by a prehistoric condor in the genus Teratornis ("monster bird"), which was also the largest flying bird that ever lived. This titan of the Pleistocene era (more than one million years ago) had a wingspan of over 23 feet (7.01 m) and weighed about 175 pounds (79.38 kg). Its remains have been found in the La Brea tar pits in Los Angeles, California.

Although vision is the best developed sense among birds, most also have fairly sharp hearing. For songbirds, hearing is obviously critical, enabling them to find a mate. Songbirds can also hear more complex sounds than we can by "slowing down" the sequence of notes to

Some species of owl, such as the great horned owl, have ear tufts at the top of the head. The ear tuft is composed of feathers. The ears, which give owls acute hearing, are located on the sides of its head.

interpret the signal. Owls also have incredible aural ability: having one ear positioned slightly lower than the other gives them "binocular hearing," enabling them to pinpoint the exact position of their prey, even in total darkness.

What range of sounds can birds hear?

Birds as a whole can hear sounds ranging from about 35 to just below 30,000 hertz (the unit of measurement of sound frequency, in which the greater the number the higher the pitch). Our range, at between 20 and 20,000 hertz, is slightly lower. Individual species, however, have a far more restricted hearing range, mostly ranging between 100 to 200 and 3000 to 18,000 hertz, though some songbirds can hear sounds as high as 29,000 hertz.

The turkey vulture uses both its keen sight and its sense of smell to locate the carrion it eats.

How well can birds smell?

Some can smell quite well. Seabirds such as storm-petrels can sniff out food sources as much as 16 miles (25 km) away. Taking advantage of this, oceangoing birders spread a foul-smelling concoction known as "chum" on the surface of the water to attract seabirds. Scavenging species such as turkey vultures also use smell to locate carrion, which may be hidden beneath the forest canopy, though the unrelated vultures of the Old World do not have a well-developed sense of smell and search for food on the open savannahs primarily by sight. Other champion sniffers include nocturnal species such as the kiwis of New Zealand, which locate their underground prey using nostrils at the tip of their bill.

Small is beautiful

The world's smallest bird is the bee hummingbird of Cuba, which weighs between 0.07 and 0.08 ounce (1.98 and 2.27 g) and measures just 2.25 inches (5.71 cm) long, half of which is bill and tail.

The title of world's smallest passerine belongs to both the black-capped and the short-tailed pygmy-tyrants of Costa Rica, which are only 2.5 inches (6.35 cm) long, while the world's smallest songbird is the pygmy tit of Java, at 3 to 3.3 inches (7.62–8.38 cm) long. The world's smallest seabird is the least storm-petrel, which breeds around the Gulf of California. It is just 5 to 6 inches (12.70–15.24 cm) long and weighs less than 1 ounce (28.3 g).

The world's smallest raptors are the falconets of Southeast Asia, including the collared, black-thighed, white-fronted and Philippine, all of which range from 5.5 to 7 inches (13.97–17.78 cm) long and weigh as little as 1.05 ounces (29.8 g).

Finally, the world's smallest flightless bird is the Inaccessible Island rail, found on the South Atlantic island of the same name. This bird is just 5 inches (12.7 cm) long and weighs just over 1 ounce (28.3 g).

What about birds' sense of touch?

In birds, this sense has been studied far less than the other senses, so much is still to be discovered. We do know, however, that some birds locate food using sensitive nerve endings in the tip of the bill or tongue: examples include shorebirds, such as snipe, which probe into mud, and woodpeckers, which extract food from beneath tree bark.

How do birds keep warm in cold weather?

In various ways. Most birds fluff out their feathers to trap an insulating layer of warm air near their body. Some also huddle together in winter roosts, taking advantage of their collective body temperature. Food is a vital factor: a hungry, underweight bird is far more likely to perish from cold than a fat healthy one!

Why don't waterbirds get frostbite?

Waterbirds such as ducks and geese sometimes face a special challenge: keeping warm while perched on ice. They do so by reducing the blood supply to their legs and feet, thus minimizing heat loss. They also have fewer nerve endings in their feet than elsewhere in their bodies, so they do not feel the effects of the cold.

SLEEP

How do birds sleep?

Quite well, though, much like us, they do so in all sorts of different ways, from brief catnaps to extended slumbers. But it is a myth that birds doze off with their head tucked beneath their wing. In fact most sleep either with their head turned back and tucked beneath their shoulder feathers or with their head slumped back onto their shoulders in a hunched position.

Where do birds sleep?

Wherever they happen to be! Perching birds usually sleep on a twig or branch (or in the case of woodpeckers, clinging to a tree trunk), waterbirds sleep either while swimming or standing on the ground and game birds sleep in dense vegetation to avoid predators. Swifts, the most aerial of birds, sleep in flight, rising high into the atmosphere to do so. Many birds gather in roosts to sleep, where they can be safer from predators and steal some warmth from others, especially in winter.

Do birds sleep standing up?

Yes, birds can sleep either standing on the ground or perched on a twig or branch. Many — especially songbirds, flamingos and shorebirds — stand alternately on one leg or the other, presumably to conserve body heat in cold weather.

When do birds sleep?

Like us, most diurnal birds sleep during the hours of darkness, when it is difficult or impossible to find food. Most nocturnal species such as owls and nightjars do the opposite and roost during daylight hours. For many groups, however, especially waterbirds such as ducks and shorebirds, sleep periods coincide with high tides when food is unavailable.

Why don't sleeping birds fall off their perches?

It is often supposed that perching birds contract their tendons automatically to prevent falling off their perch, even when fast asleep. Recent findings, though, suggest that birds may simply be very good at keeping their balance!

Do birds hibernate?

For centuries it was long believed that many migratory birds hibernated, including swallows in the mud at the bottom of ponds. But this was conclusively disproved by careful observation and banding studies in the 19th and 20th centuries. Then, in the 1940s, an incredible discovery was made: a common poorwill, a type of American nightjar, was found in a torpid state in a rock crevice in California. Studies showed that the bird was effectively in a state of hibernation, achieved by reducing its body temperature from the normal 104 degrees Fahrenheit (40°C) to 50 degrees Fahrenheit (10°C). It is now known that poorwills can maintain this state for up to a hundred days. Other groups such as hummingbirds and swifts can also shut down most of their body mechanisms to achieve a state of torpor, but for much shorter periods.

MORTALITY

How long do birds live?

Birds live from a few hours to almost as long as we do, depending on the kind of bird and the hazards it faces. Many birds die very early in their lives due to starvation or attack by predators. For birds that survive the first year, the lifespan varies depending on the species: most songbirds live for between 2 and 10 years, waders from about 5 to 10 years, and raptors from 5 to 20 or even 30 years. Parrots and seabirds are among the longest lived, with many species regularly topping 20 years and a few individuals breaking the half-century barrier. The longest surviving birds are those in captivity, which have no predators and an unending supply of food. Few wild birds will ever reach old age.

What proportion of a species' population dies each year?

Usually between one-third and two-thirds of a species die each year, though this varies from species to species and depends on environmental conditions such as a harsh winter or food shortages. Seabirds tend to have very low annual mortality rates (5 to 10 percent), while among small passerines up to three-quarters of a population may die each year.

How do birds die?

In many different ways, some natural, others due directly or indirectly to humans. Disease, lack of food and predation are the three biggest natural killers, while non-natural deaths arise from factors such as shooting, deliberate or accidental poisoning and collisions with buildings or motor vehicles. For our backyard birds, one of the biggest causes of death is predation by domestic cats. It is estimated that each year, cats are responsible for anything from 28 to 75 million bird deaths in the United Kingdom and as many as 118 million in the United States.

Do birds suffer from the same diseases as humans?

Yes, many birds suffer from avian forms of common human diseases. These include influenza, tuberculosis, botulism and salmonella. Occasionally, diseases can spread from birds to humans, as in the bacterial disease psittacosis and recent outbreaks of West Nile Virus and "bird flu," all of which can be fatal to human beings.

Why are dead birds rarely seen?

Considering that millions of birds die each year, it is amazing how few dead ones we come across. Many die out of sight of human beings, while others are killed and eaten, leaving little or no evidence of their existence. Decay and decomposition can also be very rapid, especially in warm climates.

INTELLIGENCE

How intelligent are birds?

"Bird-brained" is a very unjust insult because birds are mostly quite smart. Many signs of apparent intelligence in birds, however, such as the ability to find food or navigate over long distances, cannot really be compared with human brainpower, since much behavior is simply "programmed." Nevertheless, birds can be trained to solve quite complex problems, and some have the ability to use tools (see below).

How do birds learn to do things?

In all sorts of ways. They learn many basic life skills such as finding food by watching and imitating their parents, though instinct also plays a part. Thus male birds kept in isolation from others of their species still learn to sing, though not as well as if they had been able to hear other singing males. Birds also use a process of trial and error: if they eat an insect or plant that makes them ill, they are unlikely to do so again. Finally, birds are also capable of learning through observation of cause and effect, such as when herring gulls learn to drop a mollusk onto a hard surface to get at its contents.

Can birds count?

Not as well as we might think. The ability to count has often been ascribed to pets such as dogs, horses and intelligent birds like parrots. Experiments have shown, however, that generally this supposed ability either is a deliberate hoax by the animal's owner or reflects an unconscious reaction on the owner's part — such as relaxing when the animal reaches the "correct" number. Birds clearly know when a clutch of eggs has reached the optimum number, but this may be the result of visual perception rather than numerical ability.

Queen Mum

The world's longest-lived wild bird was a female royal albatross, banded as an adult in 1937 when she was at least 7 years old, which survived until 1990 — making her about 60 years old. The longest-lived bird in captivity was a sulphur-crested cockatoo named Cocky, which died in London Zoo, England, in 1982, aged at least 80.

Can birds solve complex problems?

It used to be thought that birds were less able to solve problems than, for example, rats and squirrels. This belief was based mainly on laboratory tests using pigeons, however, which are perhaps not the smartest of birds. Further studies have shown that some birds, especially crows and parrots, can often handle complex and multifaceted tasks, such as navigating a maze or doing steps in a particular sequence to gain a reward. But perhaps the most extraordinary example of wild birds' intelligence has been observed in Japan. In certain Japanese cities, crows deliberately place walnuts on the surface of a road when the traffic lights are red. The birds wait until the lights change, watch as a car or truck crushes the nut and then — when the lights change back to red — swoop down to pick up the nut and eat it.

Can birds use tools?

Quite a few birds use tools, usually to find food. The most famous example is the woodpecker finch of the Galápagos, which habitually uses a small twig or cactus spine to provoke an insect to emerge from a crevice or to pry it out. The New Caledonian crow goes one stage further by fashioning its own tool from a twig to use to pry grubs out of a tree trunk. Some birds that fish for a living have learned to improve their success rate by using bait. For example, the green-backed heron will drop insects or small pieces of bread onto the surface of the water to attract fish, which it can then seize with its dagger-like bill. Several species use hard objects to obtain food, either dropping stones onto eggs to break them (as one African population of Egyptian vultures does to ostrich eggs), or dropping an item of food onto a hard surface (gulls drop shellfish onto concrete and lammergeiers release bones from a great height). This behavior has passed into legend: the Greek playwright Aeschylus was reputedly killed by an eagle dropping a tortoise onto his bald head; the "eagle" is more likely to have been a lammergeier.

How did blue tits learn to open milk-bottle tops?

Between the First and Second World Wars, milk delivery companies in Britain introduced aluminum foil tops on milk bottles, which helped to keep the milk fresh when left on the customer's doorstep. It did not take long for one enterprising species, the blue tit, to discover how to get at the tasty cream inside the bottle by pecking a hole in the foil. This phenomenon was first recorded in the 1920s, and by the 1950s had spread throughout the British blue tit population. The speed at which the habit spread led some scientists to claim that this was an example of "Lamarckian evolution," in which a trick learned by the parent can be passed down to its offspring via its genes. The truth was perhaps even more astonishing: because blue tits live in family groups, the offspring were watching their parents and finding out how to pierce the foil tops by a combination of observational learning and trial and error. Interestingly, although some individual robins also learned to get into the milk bottles, the habit did not

This clever little European bird, the blue tit, learned how to open milk-bottle tops.

spread through their population and soon died out. This was because robins are mainly solitary creatures, so there was little opportunity for the skill to pass from one generation to the next. After complaints from customers, the dairy companies first tried strengthening the foil tops, but the birds simply pecked harder! Eventually, a change in packaging design and shopping habits led to a decline in doorstep milk delivery and consequently to the end of a free meal for blue tits.

Do birds have feelings?

When watching a songbird singing its heart out or a mother standing apparently forlornly over its dead chick, one can easily assume that birds have feelings very similar to our own. But to use words like "happiness" or "sadness" in relation to other members of the animal kingdom raises many questions. Lots of creatures indulge in what can be described as "play," "courtship" or "aggression," but we cannot suppose that when doing so they feel the same as we do, or even that they have the capacity to feel emotion at all. Scientists divide into two camps on this question: one side sees behavior in a purely mechanistic sense (e.g., playing is a way for young creatures to learn to hunt); the other allows the notion that birds and other animals do have emotions and feelings that, while not exactly the same as ours, have their roots in the same biological imperative. The latter approach has most eloquently been described in *The Minds of Birds* by the late American ornithologist Alexander Skutch, in which he concludes that "birds' mental capacities have been grossly underestimated ... their minds are among nature's greatest wonders."

2 WHERE DO BIRDS COME FROM?

EVOLUTION AND CLASSIFICATION

How did birds evolve?

Like every other creature on this planet, birds got here by natural selection — a process that Charles Darwin and Alfred Russel Wallace originally discovered — in which individuals with traits most suited to survival in their particular environment pass on these traits to their offspring. Such traits did not appear as the result of any preordained plan but are simply the product of tiny changes accumulated over a vast period of time. Evolution is an ongoing process, with new species continually evolving while others become extinct. So all life is in a state of constant flux. And that includes us!

Did birds evolve from dinosaurs or reptiles?

There is no doubt that birds descended from reptile-like ancestors, but the jury is still out on whether these were fully fledged dinosaurs or some other branch of the reptilian tree. Birds may have descended directly from a group called the theropod dinosaurs, which includes the intelligent, rapid and somewhat bird-like velociraptors made famous by the movie *Jurassic Park*. In recent years, however, some scientists have questioned this view, suggesting that birds descended from a different, more conventionally reptile-like ancestor.

What is the earliest known fossil bird?

Most scientists seem to agree that the first bird was the celebrated archaeopteryx, specimens of which were discovered in Bavaria in southern Germany during the 19th century. Dating from roughly 150 million years ago, the archaeopteryx appears to be the "missing link" between reptiles and birds, having a reptilian skeleton and teeth, and birdlike feathers. Other fossil discoveries, however, suggest

The archaeopteryx was a Jurassic period animal believed to be a progenitor of modern birds. A fossil was found in Germany in the mid-19th century.

that the archaeopteryx may have been an evolutionary "dead end," and there are several other contenders for the title of the world's first bird.

What is taxonomy?

Taxonomy is the study of the evolutionary relationships between different populations of animals or plants, and their classification into a great zoological filing cabinet of orders, genera, families, species and so on. It is also known as systematics.

So what is taxidermy?

Taxidermy is the craft (some would say art) of preparing the skins of birds, mammals and occasionally fish for display in a museum or private collection. Put more crudely, it is all about stuffing animals and has nothing to do with classification.

How do we know how to classify birds?

Strictly speaking, we don't. All forms of taxonomy are based on a combination of scientific knowledge and inspired guesswork. Two taxonomists rarely agree — especially about the tiny differences that separate one species from another, or when deciding where to draw the line between different genera. Several centuries

Taking orders

The largest order of birds is without question the Passeriformes (passerines), which includes almost 6,000 of the world's extant species — well over half the total.

The next largest order is the Apodiformes (swifts and hummingbirds), with about 440 species, followed by the Charadriiformes (waders, gulls etc.) and Psittaciformes (parrots, macaws and cockatoos), with about 350 species each.

There are several candidates for the smallest order of birds, depending on whose taxonomy you follow. Until recently, most authorities recognized only one order with a single species: Struthioniformes (the ostrich). However, the hoatzin, a peculiar South American bird long considered a member of the order Galliformes, has now been given its own unique order, the Opisthocomiformes. To further confuse things, some authorities now recognize two separate species of ostrich.

ago, birds were classified in terms of what they ate or their habits. Thus the osprey and the kingfisher were grouped together as "fish-eating birds," while eagles and owls were "raptors" and thought to be related to one another. Later on, by studying the insides of birds as well as their outsides, scientists created a more accurate system of classification, which more closely reflects the way birds actually evolved.

So is today's classification of birds the "true" one?

Almost certainly not. The Holy Grail of taxonomists is to trace the true evolutionary path of each species, and thus the order in which all today's species descended from a common ancestor. This process is known as phylogeny. Taxonomists can never be absolutely sure, though, that any evolutionary path is the true one because the fossil record of what actually happened is so incomplete.

What is an "order"?

In the family tree of classification, an order is the most important taxonomic category between class (e.g., birds, mammals, insects) and family (e.g., parrots, owls, buntings) (see below). There are somewhere between 23 and 28 orders, depending on whose opinion you follow. The scientific name of an order always ends in "-iformes." Orders range in size from those containing a single species, such as Opisthocomiformes (the unique hoatzin of South America), to the largest order of all, Passeriformes, which contains almost 6,000 species — over half the world's birds.

What is a "passerine"?

A passerine is a member of the order Passeriformes. Because this order is so large, it has been subdivided into two "suborders," the oscine and suboscine passerines, split according to the structure of their vocal parts. The vast majority of passerines, such as sparrows, finches, warblers, tits and larks, are oscine passerines; the suboscines include the antbirds and cotingas and are mainly confined to South America.

Are passerines the same as songbirds?

Strictly speaking, no. A songbird is a member of the oscine passerines, by far the largest grouping in the order. All passerines that regularly occur in Britain and Europe are oscine passerines, so they can be accurately described as songbirds. In North America, however, the tyrant-flycatchers (including kingbirds, phoebes and flycatchers) are suboscine passerines and so are not true songbirds, though all other North American passerines, from warblers and thrushes to sparrows and larks, are.

What is a "raptor"?

"Raptor" is generally used as a synonym for "bird of prey" and usually describes members of the order Falconiformes (eagles, hawks, buzzards, falcons etc.), and sometimes Strigiformes (owls). Defining why a bird is or is not a raptor is not always easy: some raptors do not eat meat (e.g., the palm-nut vulture), several are scavengers (e.g., Old World vultures) and some birds behave like raptors but are not (e.g., shrikes). Also excluded are birds such as gannets, even though they feed exclusively by killing other animals (in their case, fish).

What is a "shorebird"?

The term "shorebird" is used for species that belong to any of various families in the order Charadriiformes, such as plovers, sandpipers, avocets and stilts, and phalaropes. It does not apply to other families in this order, such as gulls, terns, alcids, skuas and jaegers. In Britain, and in the rest of the English-speaking world outside North America, shorebirds are generally referred to as "waders."

What are "waterfowl"?

Waterfowl (or wildfowl as they are known in Britain) are members of the order Anseriformes, that is, ducks, geese and swans.

What is a "seabird"?

Broadly speaking, the term "seabird" refers to any bird that regularly spends much of its life at sea. The term is usually confined, though, to members of the following families: tubenoses (albatrosses, shearwaters and petrels), gannets and cormorants, gulls and terns, skuas and jaegers, alcids, penguins, frigatebirds and tropicbirds. Other groups, including loons, grebes, phalaropes and certain species of duck, are not usually referred to as "seabirds," even though they may spend much of their time at sea.

What is a "family"?

In the table of classification, family is the level between order and genus. Families may contain a single species (e.g., ostrich), a dozen or more (e.g., albatrosses) or several hundred (e.g., hummingbirds, parrots, pigeons and doves). The scientific name of a family always ends in "-idae" (e.g., Parulidae — wood-warblers).

What is a "genus"?

Genus (plural: genera) falls between family and species. Effectively, a genus is a convenient grouping of closely related species, although the placing of a species within a particular genus is not always clear-cut, and the boundaries often shift. One species may be moved between genera, or one genus may be split into two or more genera — or combined with another to form a single one.

What is a "species"?

This used to be a nice simple question to answer, but thanks to recent advances in taxonomy, attempting to do so is now, frankly, a bit of a nightmare! Until recently, a species was defined as a group of birds that freely interbreed with each other but generally do not breed with other groups of birds. In practice this meant that the birds we normally recognize as being different from each other, such as blackpoll and bay-breasted warblers, or gray-cheeked and swainson's thrushes, are different species. Some apparently distinct species, however, such as the larger gulls, may appear to be separate species in one part of their range, while interbreeding in another. Moreover, populations that until now have been considered as making up a single species, such as the red crossbill, may in fact be a number of separate species — even though they are virtually indistinguishable in the field. It is important to understand that no species is fixed forever in evolutionary terms; populations constantly have the potential to mutate and eventually evolve into a separate species.

What is a "subspecies"?

A subspecies is a convenient classification of particular populations of a species into different categories. This distinction is usually applied when a population of birds in one area differs from a population of

The differences between subspecies may be obvious or very subtle, and the ranges of some subspecies may overlap.

Family affairs

The largest family of birds is the tyrant-flycatchers of the New World, comprising from 340 to more than 500 species — again, depending on whose authority you recognize. Of the nonpasserines, the largest family is either the parrots or the hummingbirds, both of which have about 320 to 350 species, closely followed by pigeons and doves, with just over 300 species.

There are many candidates for the smallest family of birds. According to James Clements' latest checklist of the world's birds, 16 nonpasserine families and 7 passerine families contain only a single species. They are ostrich, emu, hamerkop, shoebill, osprey, secretary bird, hoatzin, limpkin, kagu, sun-bittern, crab plover, ibisbill, Magellanic plover, plains-wanderer, oilbird and cuckoo-roller (nonpasserines) and sharpbill, hypocolius, palmchat, wallcreeper, bristlehead, olive warbler and bananaquit (passerines).

the same species in another area but the differences are considered too minor to warrant classifying the two populations as separate species. A good example is the division of the northern flicker *Colaptes auratus* into two subspecies: red-shafted (subspecies *cafer*), breeding in western North America, and yellow-shafted (subspecies *auratus*), breeding in eastern North America. As their names suggest, the former has reddish-brown underwings, while the latter has bright yellow ones.

What is the difference between a "race" and a "subspecies"?

There is no difference between the two terms; they are synonyms.

Do subspecies ever "graduate" to becoming full species, and vice versa?

Yes, such reclassification is referred to as "lumping" and "splitting" (see page 48).

What are "binomials"?

The system of binomial nomenclature, created more than two centuries ago by the Swedish scientist Carl Linnaeus, is still in use today. Linnaeus made the simple but revolutionary breakthrough of giving each species a unique "scientific" name, in two parts. So the house sparrow has the scientific name *Passer domesticus*, in which the first part, *Passer*, refers to the sparrow genus and is shared with two dozen or so other species, while the second part, *domesticus*, indicates that this is the house sparrow (as opposed to any other species of sparrow). Although neither the generic nor the specific name is necessarily unique, the combination of the two always is.

What's the point of binomial nomenclature?

By giving each species a unique scientific name, we can always be certain which species is being referred to. This is especially useful when different species share a common English name, such as the two unrelated species known as the black vulture, one of which is found in the New World (*Coragyps atratus*), and the other in the Old (*Aegypius monachus*). The scientific name is also very helpful when referring to a species that has different English names, for example, the bird known in North America as parasitic jaeger and in Britain as Arctic skua, but known by scientists everywhere as *Stercorarius parasiticus*.

What about "trinomials"?

Trinomials are simply an extension of the binomial concept as a means of differentiating between different subspecies (or races) of a particular species. Thus the various races of the savannah sparrow *Passerculus sandwichensis* are distinguished from each other by adding a third word to each scientific name. So the nominate race, which breeds across most of North America, is known as *Passerculus sandwichensis sandwichensis*, while the subspecies breeding on Sable Island, Nova Scotia, is known as *Passerculus sandwichensis princeps* (and is also given the name Ipswich sparrow). The repetition of the specific name as that of the subspecies indicates that the former is the so-called nominate race — that is, it was the first that scientists discovered and named.

What do "lumping" and "splitting" mean?

This is birders' slang for what happens when two formerly distinct species are reclassified as a single one (lumping), or two subspecies are given full status as separate species (splitting). In recent years splitting has become far more frequent. For example, some years ago myrtle and Audubon's warblers were "lumped" into a single species, yellow-rumped warbler, while more recently the brant (a species of goose) has been split by some people into at least three different species.

Why has lumping declined?

In recent years "lumping" — the joining together of two or more species into one — has become less frequent, partly because of the adoption by some authorities of the Phylogenetic Species Concept, as opposed to the traditional Biological Species Concept (see below). Also, as we get to know more about bird distribution, we have discovered that what we once thought were races are in fact reproductively isolated from one another and are therefore separate species.

What is the "Biological Species Concept"?

The Biological Species Concept uses the traditional way of defining species by the fact that they do not breed with other, similar species. But there are several problems with this concept. First, it is impossible to know whether two supposed species, whose ranges do not overlap, would breed with each other if their paths did cross. On the other hand, we also cannot tell whether different subspecies, whose ranges also do not overlap, would breed with each other if they got the chance or would, on the contrary, keep to their own kind. As a working definition, the Biological Species Concept creates as many problems as it solves.

What about the "Phylogenetic Species Concept"?

To try to solve these problems, some taxonomists have come up with a new system of classifying birds, the Phylogenetic Species Concept. They propose that we try to identify the smallest population of a bird that has a unique set of characteristics and consider this population to be a separate species. So, for example, every distinct race of the song sparrow would be classed as a separate species, provided we could show that its members share a definable set of characteristics.

How do scientists tell species apart using the Phylogenetic Species Concept?

With great difficulty! Any new idea is bound to be fraught with difficulties at first, and this one is no exception. Like more traditional taxonomists, scientist use a number of ways to tell species apart — from examining the internal structure and external features of a bird, to analyzing its song and using DNA analysis to compare populations.

What would happen if we adopted the Phylogenetic Species Concept?

Taken to its logical conclusion, this would create taxonomic anarchy. Instead of 700 or so regularly occurring species in North America there might be as many as several thousand — many of them only distinguishable from each other either by analyzing their sound recordings or examining them closely in the hand. Meanwhile the "world list" would increase from fewer than 10,000 species currently to more than 20,000 species. Although listers might initially be thrilled by their ever-expanding lists, they would soon become deeply frustrated by their inability to make firm identifications. Novice birders would be even more baffled and might give up altogether.

Wacky races!

The species with the largest number of subspecies is the island thrush, with 51 races currently recognized, many of them confined to tiny islands in the Pacific Ocean. The honor used to go to the golden whistler of Southeast Asia, with 64 recognized races, but this has now been split into eight different species, each with a number of different subspecies.

What are "sibling species"?

Sibling species are two or more closely related species that look similar but do not normally interbreed, even when their ranges overlap. A good example is eastern and western meadowlarks.

What are "cryptic species"?

They are two species that so closely resemble each other that telling them apart in the field is almost impossible — even though they are reproductively isolated and constitute "good" species. For example, two North American sparrows, the Nelson's sharp-tailed and saltmarsh sharp-tailed, were until recently considered to be one species, but several subtle differences in plumage, song and habitat have now led them to be split into two.

What is "adaptive radiation"?

Adaptive radiation occurs when a single group of closely related organisms, descended from a common ancestor, evolves into many different forms, usually in a relatively short time. This generally occurs when they colonize a new area — such as an island or even a continent — and evolve to fill the vacant niches available. The most famous example is Darwin's finches of the Galápagos, which, despite their very different appearances, all share a fairly recent common ancestor. The study of these birds helped Darwin form his theory of natural selection.

What is "convergent evolution"?

This occurs when two completely unrelated species or groups adopt similar characteristics due to the evolutionary pressures of sharing a similar environment. Thus the common gallinule looks superficially like a duck or a grebe because it shares their habitat and lifestyle, while its close relative the sora rail does not. Sometimes this can lead to a whole group being wrongly classified. For many years it was assumed that the New World vultures (including the California and Andean condors) were related to the Old World vultures and belonged in the order Falconiformes. In fact the condor is much more closely related to storks (Ciconiiformes). The similarities between these two groups are entirely due to their similar ecological roles as scavengers. Another good example is the extraordinary resemblance of the African longclaws (related to Old World pipits and wagtails) to the completely unrelated North American meadowlarks (related to New World orioles and blackbirds).

Are birds still evolving?

Every living species is still evolving — the process never stops! — and they are doing so much faster than we once thought. It used to be assumed that birds (and other creatures) evolved over thousands or tens of thousands of years — a far slower process than we could witness in our short lifetimes. But this assumption was shattered when studies of Darwin's finches on the Galápagos revealed evolutionary changes occurring over a few generations, covering only a decade or so. This was due to a major change in the birds' environment, brought about by the weather system known as "El Niño."

Are we still discovering new species?

Yes, both by the process of "splitting" (mainly using DNA analysis) and because every now and then a species entirely new to human knowledge is actually found in the field, having previously been undiscovered or overlooked. For example, in 2004 a new species of flightless rail was discovered on the Philippine island of Calayan. It was named, not surprisingly, the Calayan rail. New species are currently being discovered at the rate of about three per year, mostly in remote parts of South America, tropical Africa or Southeast Asia.

3 HOW MANY BIRDS ARE THERE?

POPULATION

NUMBERS

How many species of bird are there?

The answer to this question depends on who you ask, and when. Until the mid 20th century the number of bird species stood at about 8,600. Then a revolution in taxonomy — the scientific classification of living things (see Chapter 2) occurred. Using new techniques, scientists analyzed the genetic makeup of bird specimens and discovered that many so-called races (or subspecies) of birds might in fact be "proper" species. Meanwhile, there was a steady trickle of entirely new birds occasionally being discovered, mainly in South America, equatorial Africa and Southeast Asia. So by the turn of the millennium, when ornithologist James Clements published the fifth edition of his world checklist, he recognized more than 9,800 species — an increase of about one-seventh on the old figure. Some authorities go even further, recognizing well over 10,000 different species.

How does this compare to the number of other animals?

Not badly for vertebrates. There are roughly twice as many different species of bird as there are mammal species (just over 5,000) and also more birds than amphibians (roughly 6,000) and reptiles (about 8,000). However, the 9,800 or so species of bird are easily outnumbered by fish (roughly 30,000 species) and positively swamped by insects, of which there may be as many as six million — many still undiscovered.

How many species of bird have ever existed?

Estimates for the number of bird species since the archaeopteryx (thought by scientists to have been the first — see Chapter 1) range from roughly 150,000 to more than 1.5 million. This is despite the fact that only about 900 extinct birds have been identified from fossil remains, and is based on palaeontologists' theories of the rate at which species become extinct over time. The latest thinking, though, is that today's 9,800 or so bird species represent about 6 percent of all that have ever lived, giving a likely total of about 160,000 species — roughly 16 times as many as exist today.

How many species of bird are there in North America?

The most comprehensive checklist, produced by the American Ornithologists' Union (AOU) in 2004, includes 2,038 species. This covers the whole of North America and Central America, south to the boundary between Panama and Colombia, as well as Hawaii and the West Indies. As a result the AOU list contains many tropical species not found north of the Mexican border with the United States. The list generally used by North American birders, produced by the American Birding Association (ABA) excludes the area south of the U.S.-Mexican border, the West Indies and Hawaii. The latest edition (2002) contains around 930 species, less than half the number on the AOU checklist.

How many individual birds are there in the world?

In 1951, British ornithologist James Fisher estimated that there were about 100 billion individual birds in the world. If the same is true today, then birds outnumber human beings by about 15 to 1. Amazingly, nobody appears to have updated this estimate since then. This is despite considerable advances in what we know about the world's birds and the many population changes that have occurred.

How many individual birds are there in North America?

In 1956, Leonard Wing estimated that there were about 5.6 billion birds in the United States during the summer, and about 3.75 billion in winter. In 1964 James Fisher and Roger Tory Peterson updated this, estimating that by the end of the breeding season there might be as many as 20 billion individual birds in the United States alone, or almost 70 times as many birds as people! If the total world population of birds is in fact 100 billion birds (see above), then Fisher and Peterson's figure is probably an overestimate.

Breeding frenzy

The world's most numerous wild bird is the red-billed quelea. This small seed-eating bird of the weaver family is found in the dry savannah region of sub-Saharan Africa. It occurs in flocks of at least 100 million, and its total population has been estimated at several billion individuals. Quelea colonies cover several hundred hectares, and contain up to 10 million nests. Their success can be attributed to their breeding rate: pairs breed up to four times a year and take less than four weeks from laying eggs to fledging their chicks. Queleas are a major agricultural pest, and millions are killed by aerial spraying each year.

CHANGES

Do bird populations change over time?

Like all creatures, birds are subject to a wide range of external influences, from habitat loss to persecution and climate change. These affect the breeding success of individuals and, over time, the population as a whole. Within a single human lifetime, often much less, we may witness major rises and falls in bird populations. Raptors such as the peregrine declined rapidly during the 1950s and 1960s due to the use of agricultural chemicals such as DDT, but quickly recovered once these pesticides were banned. Some species have declined dramatically, such as the piping plover, which has suffered from disturbance at its nesting sites on beaches on the east coast of North America. Meanwhile others have fared much better: laughing gull numbers have risen as the species has adapted to living alongside people. Worldwide, populations of some species such as the cattle egret have positively exploded, thanks their ability to thrive alongside humans.

Rooster boosted!

The world's most numerous domesticated bird is undoubtedly the chicken, whose world population has been estimated at roughly eight billion individuals (comfortably in excess of the global human population of six billion or so people). The 175 or so domestic varieties of chicken all descend from the wild red junglefowl of Southeast Asia, which was first domesticated in India in about 3200 BC.

What causes bird populations to rise or fall?

All sorts of things. The major causes of population declines are habitat loss, persecution and pollution. Habitat loss is the biggest factor in the tropics, where illegal logging and the clearing of forests for agriculture have brought hundreds of species to the brink of extinction. Persecution is generally in decline, especially in Britain and North America, though it is still a problem in the developing world and around the Mediterranean, where many millions of migrating birds are shot each year. Pollution can have a major effect in a small area, for example, when an oil tanker runs aground (such as the 1989 *Exxon Valdez* disaster in Alaska, which killed at least 250,000 seabirds). In the future, the effects of global climate change may have profound consequences for many of the world's birds.

How do we measure these rises and falls in bird populations?

North America and Britain have a long tradition of amateur bird-watchers carrying out census and survey work. Over time they have helped give us a picture of the status, distribution and numbers of breeding and wintering birds, so we can detect changes in range or population very soon after they occur. Without the data produced by surveys such as the Summer Atlas of North American Birds, we could never be confident that these changes are actually happening, nor could we measure them so accurately.

How accurate are our estimates of bird populations?

Inevitably population estimates are a combination of hard facts and educated guesswork. Some species, such as colonially nesting seabirds, are relatively easy to survey, so population counts of species such as common murre or Atlantic puffin are probably fairly accurate. Songbirds are much harder to survey accurately; scientists organize measured counts in a particular area over a particular period, and then extrapolate from this to produce an estimate for the whole country.

Why are our songbirds declining?

In recent years many common songbird species have suffered major declines. The likeliest cause is habitat loss, especially as a result

No petrel shortage!

The world's most numerous seabird is almost certainly Wilson's storm-petrel, named after the Scottish ornithologist (and founding father of American ornithology) Alexander Wilson. This tiny seabird, weighing no more than a sparrow, can be found throughout the oceans of the southern hemisphere, as well as parts of the North Atlantic. Its oceangoing habits mean that it is rarely seen from land, so estimates of its total world population vary from a few million to tens of millions.

of intensive farming methods that reduce the amount of seed and insect food available for birds. Other causes include climate change, which may affect birds on their wintering grounds and migration routes, and the shooting and trapping of migrant birds.

Will global warming make things better or worse for birds?

That's a tricky question. In the short term, many species are likely to benefit from the effects of global warming. As spring gets earlier and earlier, however, this will have a negative effect on long-distance migrants such as the warblers, which will soon find that their arrival times have become "out of synch" with the food supply. And if conditions in South America and Central America become drier, many migrants will also suffer on their wintering grounds. Hurricanes and tropical storms are also getting more frequent and severe, as the devastation caused by Hurricane Katrina in 2005 showed.

Which birds will be affected?

Globally, the birds most under threat from global warming are those with restricted breeding and wintering ranges; just a small change in local conditions could affect such species. One example is the Kirtland's warbler, whose entire population of only a few hundred pairs breeds in the jack pine forests of northeast Michigan and winters in the Bahamas. Even tiny changes in their habitat may cause breeding failure, and the species may soon become one of the first casualties of global warming.

EXTINCTION

How many birds have become extinct in recent times?

Between the year 1600 and the late 20th century just over 80 species of bird are thought to have become extinct. These include the most famous extinct bird of all, the dodo, a large, flightless pigeon-like bird confined to the Indian Ocean island of Mauritius. The dodo died out sometime in the 17th century, partly because it was hunted for food, and partly because introduced rats and cats made short work of its eggs and chicks. Either way, people were to blame.

Scavenging for success

The world's most numerous raptor is probably the black kite, which is found in tropical and warm temperate parts of Europe, Africa, Asia and Australasia. It relies on scavenging for most of its food and has prospered thanks to our wasteful habits. In the New World the best candidate is another scavenger, the American black vulture, which can be found from Washington, D.C., to Patagonia.

Is extinction part of the natural cycle?

Up to a point, yes. Species whose populations go into long-term decline will eventually become extinct and, over time, new species will evolve to exploit vacant niches. But the pace of extinction is now much faster than ever before in recorded history, thanks largely to the spread of humankind into every corner of the world and our propensity for killing and destruction.

Has the extinction rate increased in recent years?

Yes. The extinction rate since 1600 is between 40 and 50 times what the fossil record would lead us to expect. BirdLife International recently estimated that about 1,200 species (roughly one in eight of the world's total) face the possibility of extinction during the 21st century. Without major changes to our attitudes and way of life, this grim prediction is highly likely to come true.

More than four and twenty

The most numerous bird in North America is probably red-winged blackbird, which can be found throughout much of the continent and whose total population has been estimated at more than 100 million birds.

Which bird family has suffered the most extinctions in historical times?

According to Errol Fuller, author of *Extinct Birds*, more kinds of rail — a total of 11 species — have become extinct since 1600 than any other family. They are closely followed by parrots (10 species), and pigeons and doves (10 species, if we include the dodo and its close relatives, the two species of solitaire). If we go back slightly further in time, however, we find that New Zealand's 11 species of flightless moa were all driven to extinction between the 12th century, when humans first colonized the islands, and the 17th century. The demise of the moas also spelled the end for Haast's eagle, a huge raptor weighing up to 31 pounds (14 kg), which preyed on the massive birds.

What made these families so vulnerable?

In the case of the rails, most were flightless and confined to a tiny area, often on oceanic islands where they were highly vulnerable to humans and introduced predators such as rats and cats. Several of the extinct pigeons and doves also lived on tiny oceanic islands, while the parrots have mainly become extinct through habitat loss and, more recently, the capturing of birds for the cage bird trade. The moas were simply hunted to extinction for food; being flightless probably didn't help them.

Have any North American birds become extinct in historical times?

Yes. Five species have definitely become extinct — the great auk (the last verifiable North American record was in 1841), Labrador duck (1875), passenger pigeon (1899) Carolina parakeet (1904, though a few almost certainly survived into the 1920s or even 1930s) and Bachman's warbler (1962) — along with two distinctive races, the heath hen (1932) and the dusky seaside sparrow (1987). Another species, the Eskimo curlew, is almost certainly extinct now, though optimistic birders continue to search for it!

The extinction of a bird as numerous as the passenger pigeon once was is difficult to fathom. The species was so abundant that migrating flocks are reported to have contained a billion or more birds!

Hero to zero

The most numerous bird that ever existed was probably the passenger pigeon, whose population (confined to North America) may have reached 10 billion individuals, though a figure of 3 billion is more likely. This sociable bird traveled in vast flocks, sometimes containing many millions of birds, which blocked out the sun for hours on end. At its peak, the passenger pigeon population may have accounted for between one-quarter and one-half of all North America's birds. Yet by 1899 the species was extinct in the wild, probably as a result of persecution and habitat loss. The last captive bird, a female named Martha, died in Cincinnati Zoo in September 1914. She is now on display at the U.S. National Museum in Washington, D.C., testament to the destructive folly of humankind.

What caused these species to become extinct?

In the case of the great auk, Labrador duck, passenger pigeon and Eskimo curlew, hunting for food appears to have been the main cause of their demise. The Carolina parakeet is a puzzle: it appeared to be highly adaptable, but nevertheless went rapidly extinct sometime during the early 20th century. One suggestion is that being highly colonial birds, they succumbed to disease. The other species suffered from habitat loss: all were highly specialized and simply could not survive the impact of human beings on their lifestyle.

How do we know when a species has become extinct?

We don't. As a bird gets more and more rare, the number of sightings dwindles to a trickle, until eventually some time has passed since the last verifiable record. Often the picture is confused by unauthenticated reports, as people eager to see a rare species claim to have sighted it. Thus the last definite sighting of the Eskimo curlew in the United States was in Texas in April 1963, though another bird was shot in Barbados later that year. Since then several sightings have been claimed, but the relevant authorities have confirmed none of them. Occasionally we assume that we have found the very last wild bird alive, as in the case of Spix's macaw, which inhabited a small area of northeastern Brazil, the only suitable habitat for the species. For several years, a lone male was seen, often tagging along with parrots of another species for company. Sadly, ornithologists visiting the area in late 2000 could not find him, despite a thorough search. We can only assume that he had finally died, unable to find a mate.

Have any "extinct" birds been rediscovered?

In 1986 ornithologists in northern India stumbled across a Jerdon's courser, a nocturnal wading bird that had not been seen since the early 1900s and had long been presumed extinct. Using a powerful flashlight they dazzled the bird, enabling one of the observers to walk over and pick it up! Even more remarkably, the four-colored flowerpecker was rediscovered on the Philippine island of Cebu in 1992, 87 years after it had last been seen. The flowerpecker is now confined to a tiny remnant of a forest that once covered 11,000 hectares, and the bird is likely to become extinct during the next few years. Most amazing of all, the New Zealand storm-petrel, last seen alive in 1850, was rediscovered in 2004, having survived undetected for more than 150 years. It is now seen regularly off the coast of New Zealand.

Which species has made the greatest comeback?

Apart from those considered extinct and then rediscovered, several species have come back from the brink of extinction, with only a handful of individuals remaining in the wild. They include Mauritius kestrel (down to nine individuals in 1973, but now numbering in the hundreds) and the Chatham Islands black robin. This little bird, found on an island off New Zealand, was down to five

Going, going ...

The world's rarest bird is a title with many contenders, as it is impossible to know when a particular species is down to a single individual. Until recently, the chief contender was Spix's macaw, with a single male left in the wild until sometime in the year 2000. A handful of individuals are still kept in captivity, however, so the bird is not yet completely extinct, though probably it is doomed to be so. After the last wild Spix's macaw died, the title of the world's rarest bird passed to a Hawaiian honeycreeper, the po'ouli. In September 2004 one of the last three wild birds was captured in the hope of starting a captive breeding program, but the bird died on November 24. The remaining two birds were last seen in February 2004 and may in fact now be no more.

birds by 1980, with just a single breeding pair — nicknamed "Old Blue" and "Old Yellow." Fortunately they managed to breed. Today's population of about 300 birds is entirely descended from those two! Less lucky was Stephens Island wren, from Cook Strait in New Zealand, whose entire population was caught and killed by the cat belonging to the island's lighthouse-keeper.

How many species are currently at risk of extinction?

At the turn of the third millennium, BirdLife International published *Threatened Birds of the World*, which included 1,186 species considered at risk (an increase of 75 on the 1994 total). Of these, 182 species are classed as "critical," meaning that they have only a slim chance of surviving the next decade or so. Another 321 are classed as "endangered," while the remaining 680 or so are classed as "vulnerable." Just as worryingly, a further 727 species are considered "near threatened." Altogether, this means that one in five of the world's bird species gives cause for concern.

Some birders and ornithologists believe that the ivory-billed woodpecker, which was thought to be extinct, may still survive in very small numbers in remnant swamp forests of the southeastern United States.

Back from the brink!

In early 2005 it was announced that a truly iconic North American bird had been rediscovered in February 2004 after being thought lost forever. The ivory-billed woodpecker had been on the verge of being declared extinct, with the last reliable sightings in the United States in 1944 and the last report of the Cuban subspecies in 1987. Then, following a number of tantalizingly brief glimpses in the forests of Arkansas, a bird was finally captured on video, and the survival of the species could be officially confirmed. Large tracts of potential habitat still exist in the region and, provided that a viable population still exists, there is hope that this flagship species can be saved.

Which continent or country has the most species at risk?

South America and Asia have the most species of bird, so it is perhaps not surprising that they also have the most at risk of extinction. Within these continents, Brazil and Indonesia are the worst cases, each with more than 100 species giving serious cause for concern. The Philippines and New Zealand have the highest proportion of threatened species, with 15 percent at risk of extinction. But the worst of all is Hawaii, where one-third of all native bird species are currently at risk of extinction.

Does North America have any species at risk of extinction?

Yes. North America has a number of species in the endangered category, including two of the continent's largest and most famous birds, the whooping crane and the California condor, as well as the ivory-billed woodpecker, which was recently rediscovered after an absence of almost 60 years. One observer compared this event to finding Elvis Presley alive and well!

4 WHERE DO BIRDS LIVE?

DISTRIBUTION

Are birds found everywhere?

Pretty much. Birds have conquered virtually everywhere it is possible for life to survive, apart from the ocean depths and the upper reaches of the atmosphere. They breed on every one of the world's seven continents, even in the heart of Antarctica, and can survive the most extreme habitats, from remote islands and the open ocean to landlocked deserts and barren mountaintops. In the past century or so they have even moved into our cities, as in the example of the feral pigeon, who deliberately moved to live right alongside us to take advantage of new food supplies and places to nest. Everywhere we have been — apart from outer space — birds go too.

Where do the most birds live?

Although birds are found throughout the world, the number of species varies enormously from one region to another. Broadly speaking, there are more birds the closer you get to the equator, with the tropics having the greatest variety and the polar regions the least. But despite having far less variety, the Arctic and Antarctic regions still support huge populations of certain species.

What are "faunal areas"?

Scientists have divided the world into six faunal areas (also known as zoogeographic regions): Palearctic, covering Europe, North Africa, the Middle East and Asia north of the Himalayas; Nearctic (North America north of the tropics); Neotropical (Central and South America); Afrotropical (sub-Saharan Africa); Oriental (Southeast Asia and the Indian subcontinent); and Australasian (the area east of a boundary known as "Weber's Line," comprising eastern Indonesia, New Guinea, Australia and New Zealand). The world's oceans, oceanic islands and Antarctica are not included in any of these regions.

What is the "Holarctic"?

"Holarctic" is the name given to the Nearctic and Palearctic regions combined. A number of circumpolar species, such as the red knot, have a Holarctic breeding range.

Packing them in

The country with the highest number of recorded species is, by a whisker, Colombia, with 1,795, closely followed by Peru (1,780), Brazil (1,701), Ecuador (1,589) and Indonesia (1,549). Six of the 12 countries with over 1,000 species are in South America. The United States is in 18th position, just ahead of Panama but below Angola.

Which regions have the most species?

The most bird-rich regions — at least in terms of the number of species — are the zones that cover the tropical and equatorial areas of the world, that is, Neotropical, Afrotropical and Oriental. For example, the Neotropical region contains about 3,000 species (roughly 30 percent of the world's total), while the Palearctic and Nearctic regions have only about 1,000 and 750 species, respectively. Despite its smaller size, the Australasian region contains about 1,600 species, many of which are found only in that part of the world.

Which habitat supports the greatest variety of species?

Undoubtedly the tropical rainforest, which supports a greater variety of all animal life than any other habitat. Found across parts of South America, equatorial Africa and Southeast Asia, this is also one of the world's most threatened habitats, due to pressures from human exploitation. As a result, many rainforest species are at risk of extinction.

The Latin Quarter

The most bird-rich continent is undoubtedly South America, where at least 2,500 species live, more than one-quarter of all the species in the world.

Which habitat supports the smallest variety of species?

The two polar areas, especially Antarctica, which has only a handful of regularly occurring breeding species, most of them penguins. Many more species, however, breed in the sub-Antarctic islands such as the Falklands, South Georgia and Snares Island, off the southern coast of New Zealand.

What is a "montane" species?

This term applies to a species that normally lives and breeds in mountainous areas. In North America birds such as the Clark's nutcracker and the mountain chickadee are considered to be montane species, generally living at above 9,800 feet (3,000 m). Montane species are usually altitudinal migrants, moving down to lower altitudes in winter to find food.

What is a "riparian" species?

One normally found along rivers and streams, such as the American dipper, which is confined to this habitat because it feeds by plunging beneath the surface of fast-flowing water to obtain its invertebrate

Continental thrift

The least bird-rich continent is Antarctica, which, despite being roughly twice the size of Australia, has only about 45 species, only 11 or so of which breed there. Many other seabird species, however, can be found in the oceans around the continent.

food. The world's four species of dipper have evolved a specialized lifestyle perfectly suited to this unique habitat.

What is a "pelagic" species?

This refers to oceangoing seabirds that spend most of their lives at sea, usually coming to land only to breed or when driven ashore by very bad weather. Pelagic species include alcids, gannets and boobies, frigatebirds and, to a lesser extent, gulls, terns, cormorants, phalaropes, loons and penguins. But the birds best suited to the oceanic lifestyle are undoubtedly the tubenoses — the 120 or so species of albatrosses, petrels, storm-petrels and shearwaters that are perfectly adapted to living for long periods at sea. The "tubenose" is a protuberance on top of their bill that allows them to smell food from many miles away, and to excrete excess salt from drinking seawater.

What is a "cosmopolitan" species?

This is any species that breeds over much of the globe, including both the Old World and the New World, as opposed to most other species, which are confined to just one or two of the world's regions. Examples include the osprey, peregrine falcon, barn owl, cattle egret and — by virtue of extensive introductions — house sparrow.

What is a "relict" species?

A relict species is one that was once found over a wide geographical area but is now confined to a relatively small part of its former range. Sometimes two populations have ended up isolated from one another, perhaps thousands of miles apart. The azure-winged magpie is found in China and Japan and has a completely separate population in Spain and Portugal. It used to be thought that explorers had brought this species back to western Europe. Fossil evidence now suggests that it once occurred naturally right across Europe and Asia but has disappeared from all but the westernmost and easternmost extremities of its former range. Another example is the Caspian tern, whose range extends over much of the Old and New Worlds yet is highly fragmented, with scattered colonies located many hundreds of miles apart.

Where the rare things are

The country with the most species with a restricted range (defined by BirdLife International as being less than 19,300 square miles (50,000 km2) is Indonesia, with 407 species.

What is an "endemic" species?

An endemic species is one confined to a restricted geographical area. This area could be a faunal region, a country or even just a single island, depending on how you wish to define it. An endemic species may thus be very widespread or very localized. So despite being the world's most common bird and found across much of sub-Saharan Africa, the red-billed quelea can still be categorized as an African endemic. At the other extreme, the Razo lark is confined to a tiny island in the Cape Verde archipelago, with fewer than 100 individuals in an area of less than 2.7 square miles (7 km^2).

Does the United States have any endemic species?

Yes, the continental United States has up to 10 endemics, depending on which taxonomy is followed: black rosy-finch, brown-capped rosy-finch, California condor, Florida scrub-jay, Island scrub-jay, lesser prairie chicken, Gunnison sage-grouse, McKay's bunting, red-cockaded woodpecker and yellow-billed magpie. Of these, the California condor and red-cockaded woodpecker are also classified as

The California condor was once on the verge of extinction but in recent decades has been the focus of intensive recovery efforts. Small numbers of California condors now live in isolated locations in California, Arizona and Baja California, Mexico.

"threatened" species. The now extinct Carolina parakeet was also endemic to the United States. If Hawaii, which lies outside the Nearctic region, is included, there are a further 33 endemic species, and 17 extinct ones in the United States.

Which region has the most endemic families?

The region with the most endemic families is, not surprisingly, the Neotropical region, with 31, though the Australasian region has 16 families found nowhere else in the world. By contrast, the Palearctic has just one endemic family (the accentors), while the Nearctic has none.

Why do endemic species occur?

Most endemic species are found in specific hotspots, known as "areas of endemism." These include oceanic islands, mountainous regions and some lowland habitats such as tropical forests. The common factor is that at some time in the distant past their birdlife was isolated from that in other, similar areas — either by the sea or by natural barriers of unsuitable habitat such as grassland. As a result, isolated populations eventually evolved into species different from their counterparts elsewhere. Endemism in birds often goes hand in hand with that in groups of plants and animals — as in Madagascar, where a largely unique fauna and flora have evolved, including the famous lemurs, as well as endemic bird families such as the vangas and mesites.

Bird-free zones

The country with fewest species is the Pacific Island of Nauru, with between 24 and 27, depending on which taxonomy is followed. Easter Island, also in the Pacific Ocean, has only nine breeding species but is not a sovereign state so cannot strictly be counted as a "country." Both islands were devastated at the hand of man — Nauru by phosphate mining and Easter Island by deforestation — so it is not surprising they are so poor for birds. If breeding species alone are counted, Vatican City probably has the fewest, though if "flyovers" are counted, its national list is undoubtedly longer than that of either of the Pacific islands.

Why do some islands have lots of endemics, while others have very few?

Islands that have been isolated for several million years tend to have more endemics than those that until recently were connected to another landmass. So Jamaica has about 27 endemic species, including four hummingbirds, two parrots and a wood-warbler, while

Chilled out

The most southerly bird is the aptly named South Polar skua, which has been sighted at the Russian base at Vostok in Antarctica. This is officially the coldest place in the world, where temperatures have dropped as low as minus 128.6 degrees Fahrenheit (−89.2°C). The world's hardiest bird, however, is surely the emperor penguin. It not only spends its whole life on the Antarctic ice, but also chooses to breed in winter, when temperatures can drop lower than minus 49 degrees Fahrenheit (−45°C). No wonder polar explorer Apsley Cherry-Garrard described his quest to find breeding emperor penguins as "the worst journey in the world."

The most southerly breeding bird is, perhaps surprisingly, not the emperor penguin, but the Antarctic petrel, which has been recorded nesting at latitude 80°30′ south.

nearby Trinidad has only one, the Trinidad piping-guan. This is because Jamaica has existed independently for millions of years, while Trinidad was connected to the South American continent until only a few thousand years ago.

What is the difference between range and distribution?

Often there is no difference. Both terms are commonly used to refer to the area in which a bird breeds, spends the winter or passes through during migration. But distribution can also refer to the more precise spacing of a bird's population within its range.

Do some birds' ranges change over time?

Yes. Just like rises and falls in bird populations, changes in range frequently occur, and for all sorts of different reasons. Expansions, when a species colonizes a new area, may arise from climate change, a new food source or human intervention — either deliberate or accidental. Likewise, contractions may result from many factors, including persecution, loss of habitat and climate change.

How far can a species expand its range?

There's no stopping certain species. If the conditions are right, some even manage to reach new continents. The classic case is the collared dove, which during the 20th century spread north and west from its original breeding range in southwest Asia to colonize virtually the whole of Europe, and has now gained a foothold in the New World too — though it may have had a helping hand to get there. The original impulse to explore new areas was probably the result of a genetic mutation, but the reason for the birds' success was finding a vacant ecological niche, which they were able to exploit. Another example is the brown-headed cowbird, which in recent years has spread east from the prairies to colonize much of North America, to the detriment of many songbirds (the species lays its eggs in other birds' nests). The cattle egret is the only species that has spread naturally from the Old to the New World in historical times, having reached South America from West Africa following a storm in the early 20th century.

Do people influence changes in the range of bird species?

As we continue to rearrange Earth's surface to suit our own ends, so we exert a disproportionate influence over the populations and distribution of birds. This is not a recent phenomenon: neolithic humans cleared forests to plant crops, thus presumably benefiting grassland species at the expense of forest ones. But during the late 20th century, the effects on the environment began to have a far greater impact. Modern agriculture, road and house building, pollution and persecution have all eaten deeply into the range of many species.

Which species have been the biggest losers?

The biggest losers have been specialized birds such as the ivory-billed woodpecker, driven to almost inevitable extinction by the felling of large tracts of mature forest in the southern part of the

Feeders have altered the migration habits of many species and in some cases extended their range. Populations of cardinals are now more common in urban areas than in the wild and stay year round because of the thousands of backyard feeders people maintain.

United States. Conservationists fear that its smaller relative the red-cockaded woodpecker may be next to disappear; once found widely in pine woods throughout the southern states, it has retreated into tiny "islands" of habitat, and without radical conservation measures its future looks bleak.

Are some birds more adaptable than others?

Yes. Many birds have learned to live alongside human beings, and some resourceful species have positively flourished in our company. For example, "seagulls" have long since ceased to live exclusively on the coast and now nest on high-rise buildings in cities, where they find rich pickings among what we leave behind. Other examples include peregrines and red-tailed hawks nesting on skyscrapers in Manhattan, and various kinds of parakeet that thrive in city parks from London to Miami.

On top of the world

The title of the most northerly bird is shared by three species — black-legged kittiwake, snow bunting and northern fulmar — each of which has been seen at the North Pole itself. The most northerly breeding bird is the ivory gull, which has been found nesting on the edge of the Arctic pack ice at latitude 85° north.

What is a "monotypic" species?

One with a single race across its entire range. One example is the short-toed eagle, which breeds in Europe, northwest Africa and Asia but whose populations do not vary enough from one another to be separated as different subspecies.

Do species vary across their geographical range?

Sometimes. Species of which one population shows consistently distinct characteristics from another population elsewhere in its range are known as "polytypic," with two or more different races

A bird's world

Two species vie for the title of world's most widespread wild bird — the Arctic tern and the cattle egret — both of which have been recorded on all seven continents. The cattle egret colonized Australia from Asia, and North America from Africa (via South America). Wilson's storm-petrel is found over most of the world's southern oceans, though is less common north of the equator. Several waders, notably the sanderling and the ruddy turnstone, are found on most of the world's coasts, from the Americas and Europe to Africa, Asia and Australia.

The world's most widespread passerine is the barn swallow, which occurs on every continent apart from Antarctica. The horned (or shore) lark also has a vast breeding range, spanning North America, Europe, northwest Africa and Asia; a tiny population inhabits the Andes.

being recognized (see Chapter 2). Examples include the Winter wren, which has 13 recognized races in the Western Palearctic alone, and several more in North America. These may vary considerably in appearance: the Alaskan race is up to one-fifth larger than its more southerly relatives. Many races occur on remote offshore islands, of which the most famous is the St. Kilda Wren, which is slightly larger, darker and longer-billed than its counterpart on the Scottish mainland.

What is a "cline"?

Not all birds can be neatly classified into distinctive subspecies; many vary gradually from one end of their range to another, for example, getting smaller or larger, darker or lighter. This phenomenon is known as a cline and occurs most frequently in colonial seabirds.

What does "indigenous" mean?

An indigenous species is simply one that has evolved naturally to live in a particular area, without having been introduced there by human agency. In other words, an indigenous species is a native one. If a species expands its range as an indirect result of human activity, such as the clearing of forests, it is still considered indigenous to that area. But if humans have deliberately or accidentally introduced it, then it is not considered indigenous. For example, in North America the gray partridge is a non-native species, having been brought from Europe. Conversely, in Britain the Common pheasant and red-legged partridge are non-native species, having been introduced for the purpose of shooting, while the much rarer gray partridge is a native species.

What is a "naturalized" species?

One that, having been introduced by human agency (either deliberately or not), has now established a fully self-sustaining population. The distinction between "naturalized," "introduced" and "feral" is not always clear. Many people use them interchangeably, although strictly speaking only "introduced" implies a deliberate release.

Birds with altitude

The bird recorded at the highest altitude on land is the alpine (or yellow-billed) chough, a small group of birds that followed a climbing expedition to a height of 26,500 feet (8,077 m) on Mount Everest in 1924. They survived by foraging on scraps of the climbers' food as they went. The alpine chough has also been recorded nesting in the Himalayas at altitudes of up to 19,500 feet (5,944 m) above sea level. The lowest altitude at which birds have been recorded is the Dead Sea depression in Israel, where little green bee-eaters have been found nesting at almost 1,300 feet (396 m) below sea level.

Does "alien" mean the same as "introduced" or "naturalized"?

In practice, yes. The word "alien," however, has negative cultural associations due in part to its link with invaders from outer space and

Home made

The country with the most endemic species is, according to ornithologist James Clements, Australia, with 238 endemics. The island of New Guinea (which comprises two states, Papua New Guinea and Irian Jaya), however, has 330 endemics. The country with the highest proportion of endemics is Madagascar, where endemics account for more than one in three of all bird species. New Guinea also has an extraordinarily high rate of endemism, with almost half of all species native to the island. More than 130 countries have no endemics at all. The countries with the lowest proportion of endemics are Guyana and Ghana, with none, despite each having more than 700 species on their national lists.

more recently its use to describe illegal immigrants. Thus conservationists try to avoid the word, preferring more neutral alternatives such as "exotic" or "non-native."

What is a "feral" species?

A feral species is one that is now living freely in a wild state, having either escaped or been released from captivity. Such a species is often regarded as halfway between tame and wild, and "feral" ceases to apply when a population has become entirely self-sustaining. The monk parakeet is no longer regarded as feral in the United States, whereas several other species of escaped parrot are still described as such because their populations have yet to become fully established.

What is a "reintroduced" species?

A reintroduced species is one that was once indigenous to a particular area or country, then died out, but has now been returned to the wild with human intervention. The best-known example is the California condor, whose entire population was removed from the wild, bred in captivity and released back into parts of its former range. This was a controversial but ultimately successful scheme, which almost certainly saved this magnificent bird from extinction.

Why are birds introduced into a new area?

Introductions are not always deliberate: exotic cage birds often escape and, while most fail to survive in their hostile new environment, a few thrive and establish self-sustaining breeding populations. Another common reason for introducing birds to a new area is for game: this accounts for the presence of several exotic gamebirds in the United States, including the ring-necked pheasant, a southwest Asian species, and even the Himalayan snowcock! Finally, some birds have been introduced purely for their aesthetic value, including the European starling, released in Central Park in the 19th century by a misguided philanthropist who believed every bird mentioned in Shakespeare should be found in the United States. Today, starlings can be found from Alaska to Baja California and almost everywhere in between.

Which introduced birds are most likely to do well?

Parrots have a good record in this respect — especially the smaller parakeets, whose adaptable behavior and gregarious habits enable them to gain a rapid foothold. Monk parakeets, from South America, have thriving colonies in parts of the United States, from Florida to Connecticut, and in several European cities including Barcelona. Crows are also highly adaptable: the Indian house crow has hitched a ride on ships to many places, including the Netherlands, the Red Sea resort of Eilat in Israel and even Durban, South Africa.

Which area has had the most introductions?

The two places that have had the most species introduced into their avifauna are Hawaii, with over 160 species, and New Zealand, with more than 130 — including such familiar British birds as the song thrush, Common blackbird and European goldfinch. However, the Miami area of Florida probably has more exotic species living in a semi-wild state than any comparable area, as escaped tropical

World beater

The most successful introduced bird is probably the humble house sparrow, which originally was found only in Europe and parts of Asia and North Africa. House sparrows have been successfully (or disastrously, depending on your point of view) introduced to North America, South Africa, New Zealand and many island groups — including the Falklands and Hawaii. Today the house sparrow occupies an area of land equivalent to about one-quarter of Earth's land surface.

parrots and other birds thrive on the area's warm climate and plentiful supply of food.

Which is the most bizarre introduction?

There are several candidates, but surely the most incongruous introduction is exemplified by a small colony of the greater bird-of-paradise, originally from New Guinea, on the island of Little Tobago in the Caribbean. Originally introduced there by a wealthy English newspaper proprietor in 1909, the birds managed to survive until a major hurricane wiped out much of their habitat in 1963, which led to an irreversible decline. The last bird was seen in 1981.

5 HOW DO BIRDS MOVE?

LOCOMOTION

IN THE AIR

Are birds the only animals that can fly?

Obviously not, since millions of insects also fly. But birds reign supreme among vertebrates (animals with backbones — also including mammals, reptiles, amphibians and fish). In fact the only other vertebrates capable of powered flight (as distinct from gliding, as practiced by certain "flying" squirrels, fish, frogs, lizards and snakes) are bats, and they have evolved nothing like the variety of forms and techniques that birds have. Just think of the completely different ways in which, say, eagles, hummingbirds, albatrosses, ducks and larks take to the sky, and you will begin to appreciate birds' amazing mastery of the air. As the great bird artist Roger Tory Peterson put it, "Birds have wings — they travel."

What make birds so good at flying?

Well, apart from wings and feathers (see Chapter 1), birds' other important adaptations include thin, hollow bones and a lack of heavy teeth and jaws, which help reduce their body weight. They also have a highly efficient blood circulation and respiratory system and a high metabolic rate, which increase their ability to convert energy into flying power.

How did flight evolve?

In birds, the ability to fly is inextricably linked to the evolution of feathers. Their lightness, strength and aerodynamic shape were the key to getting birds into the air. It seems most likely that the earliest birds first developed feathers on their wings and tail, which enabled them to glide for short periods. As the development of a full set of feathers progressed, the descendants of these ancestral birds were able to fly farther, higher and for longer periods. Natural selection gave the best flyers the highest chances of survival. So over many, many generations — covering hundreds of thousands, perhaps millions of years — flight evolved. It eventually became birds' standard means of getting around.

How do birds get airborne?

The first challenge birds have is getting airborne. To do this, a bird has to overcome the force of gravity by generating enough energy to lift itself into the air and stay there. Small birds are light enough to simply flap their wings and take off, but larger ones such as ducks and geese may have to build up forward motion by running or flapping across the surface of the water. Really heavy birds, such as bustards and swans, must put in even more effort over an even greater distance to become airborne.

How do birds stay airborne?

Once a bird is up in the air, its next challenge is to stay there. To do so it must overcome the problem of drag that results from its own forward motion. A bird does this by generating enough lift to overcome drag and reach an equilibrium. The laws of physics mean that the faster a bird flies, the less drag it generates, so fast-flying birds use less energy over the same distance than slower ones do. Different species use very different methods to stay in the air. Some generate lift by flapping their wings rapidly; others use long or broad wings for gliding; heavier species such as raptors soar on broad wings, taking advantage of rising air currents such as thermals (see page 88).

How long can a bird stay airborne?

In some cases, almost as long as it wants. Several birds, including swifts, albatrosses and the sooty tern, are known to spend almost unimaginably long periods on the wing without ever landing; indeed they touch down eventually only because no bird can lay eggs and raise young in mid-air! Swifts can feed, sleep and even copulate while in flight, testament to the incredible adaptability of birds.

How high do birds fly?

Birds fly at altitudes of just above sea level to 10,000 (3000 m) feet or more, depending on the species and whether it is traveling a short distance or undertaking a long migratory journey. Most birds seldom have any cause to rise above 1,600 feet (500 m) or so. But extra-efficient respiration, plus the ability to survive extremely cold temperatures, allows some birds to reach extraordinary altitudes. Vultures, swans and geese have been recorded flying at jet airliner heights, in conditions that no mammal could possibly survive.

The sky's the limit

The world's most airborne bird is probably the sooty tern, which may not land for an amazing seven or more years after leaving the colony where it was born. The common swift is also highly adapted to an aerial existence, with some individuals not touching down for at least 18 months between fledging and first breeding, during which time they will have migrated from Europe to Africa and back — twice! Both these birds sleep and feed on the wing, the swift snapping up tiny flying invertebrates, and the tern snatching morsels of food from the waves.

What is "wing-loading"?

This technical term takes us into the territory of flight engineers. Essentially, wing-loading is the ratio between the wing area and the weight of the bird; thus, the greater a bird's wing area in relation to its weight, the lower its wing-loading. Birds with a low wing-loading, such as vultures and condors, are able to soar for long periods without flapping their wings and using up energy; birds with a high wing-loading, such as swans and geese, must flap their wings constantly. The group of birds with the lowest wing-loading of all is the frigate-birds, which can hang in the air almost effortlessly for hours or days on end. In fact, these enormous seabirds are so light that their skeleton actually weighs less than their feathers.

How many different flight techniques do birds use?

As well as the standard means of flapping their wings, birds have developed several more specialized techniques to stay airborne or reduce the expenditure of energy. These include gliding — using out-stretched wings to travel forward without flapping (e.g., sharp-shinned hawk); soaring — similar to gliding but generally in a circling pattern, using air currents to gain or maintain lift (e.g., red-tailed hawk); and hovering — flapping wings very rapidly to stay in one place for a short period of time (e.g., American kestrel). Basic wing shape means that every species tends to favor a particular technique. But wings are adjustable, and most birds will adapt to suit the conditions. For example, hawks sometimes soar, while buzzards often glide and sometimes even hover!

In a flap

The smaller hummingbirds are the birds with the fastest wingbeat, which has been measured at between 70 and 90 beats per second. Recent improvements in technology, however, have allowed even more accurate measurements, revealing that a displaying male ruby-throated hummingbird can reach a rate of an amazing 200 beats per second. The birds with the slowest wingbeat are probably the albatrosses, which can glide for days over the open oceans without flapping their wings at all, using air currents rising from the surface to stay airborne.

Why do some species glide, soar or hover?

Gliding and soaring are mainly practiced by larger, heavier birds such as eagles, hawks and gulls so that they can stay airborne longer (an advantage when searching for food over a large area). Seabirds such as albatrosses and shearwaters ("stiff-wings") practice "dynamic soaring." This is a technique that enables them to glide great distances over the ocean's surface without flapping, even in windless conditions, by using the updraft from wave slopes. Both soaring and gliding conserve energy. Hovering, by contrast, tends to use a lot of energy for a very brief period. It allows a bird to remain stationary in mid-air, however, enabling, for example, a falcon to spot prey in the grass below or a hummingbird to sip nectar from flowers.

Do birds ever fly backward?

The only group of birds whose members regularly fly backward is the hummingbirds. They have evolved a special flight technique, involving flexible shoulder joints and extremely fast wing beats, which enables them to move in any direction — forward, sideways, up, down or backward — to position themselves perfectly for sipping nectar from a hanging flower. Other birds occasionally fly backward for very brief periods, either accidentally, when caught by the wind, or deliberately, to avoid attack or catch their prey.

Can birds fly upside down?

No birds habitually fly upside down, though some birds may do so for very brief periods by accident. A few will also flip or roll over during aerial courtship displays, including various raptors and — of course — rollers.

How fast do birds usually fly?

Flying speeds vary considerably, depending on the group or species involved and whether it is on a short flight or a long migratory journey. Most migrating songbirds fly at speeds of between 15 and 25 miles per hour (25–40 km/h), which is the optimum range for balancing the expenditure of energy and the distance covered. Larger birds often fly faster: cruising speeds for shearwaters and albatrosses are about 25 to 35 miles per hour (40–55 km/h), while ducks, geese and swans can maintain speeds of up to 44 to 47 miles per hour (70–75km/h) over long distances. Ironically, one bird named for its speed, the common swift, is in fact rather slow: it generally flies at between 14 and 25 miles per hour (23–40km/h), though it is supremely agile and maneuverable.

What are thermals?

Thermals are rising columns of warm air, produced by the radiant heat of the sun on Earth's surface. They generally occur from mid-morning onward, as the sun rapidly raises the temperature of the cooler ground. Large, heavy birds such as vultures and buteos use thermals to gain height as quickly as possible without expending valuable energy by flapping. Once they have reached their desired altitude, they will then glide away toward a new feeding area. Thermals are also important for many raptors and other large birds during migration, especially when they are about to cross a wide expanse of water.

How does the weather affect flying birds?

Weather is sometimes a help, sometimes a hindrance and sometimes downright fatal to birds. As well as using thermals to gain height or air currents over the open ocean for "dynamic soaring" (see page 87), many migratory birds use particular weather conditions to aid them in their journey. For example, light following winds that high-pressure systems produce in spring help carry northbound migrants to their destination more quickly. Bad weather, on the other hand, is a huge obstacle to migrating birds, many of which will perish if caught in a hurricane or tropical storm.

How does rough weather affect migrants?

Migrating birds are at the mercy of the elements. Unusually windy or stormy weather may drive many off their intended course, some-

Birds of prey such as vultures and eagles are champion riders of "thermals," or warm air currents. During migration, mixed "kettles" of these birds can be seen soaring on high overhead. Expert birders can identify by species what seem to be mere specks in the sky.

times with unexpected results. Every autumn, millions of North American landbirds head out into the Atlantic Ocean on their journey south, but strong winds — especially in the aftermath of a hurricane — may push them eastward. The vast majority of these

Speed freaks

The world's fastest flying bird is probably the peregrine falcon, whose speed during its "stooping" dive has been claimed to exceed 190 miles per hour (300 km/h), though more accurate measurements suggest that it is closer to 112 miles per hour (180 km/h).

The white-throated needletail (a type of swift from Asia) has been recorded flying at 106 miles per hour (170 km/h). In level flight, the record is held by the eider duck, whose flight has been reliably measured at 47.5 miles per hour (76.4 km/h), though another duck, the red-breasted merganser, has been reported to reach speeds of over 80 miles per hour (129 km/h) when in escape flight.

displaced birds will become exhausted and perish in the waves, but a few will cross the Atlantic and make landfall in Britain or Ireland.

Why are some birds flightless?

Given that flying is virtually synonymous with birds, it does seem odd that a few cannot do it at all. But in fact flightlessness can make perfect sense as long as it confers benefits that will give the individual an evolutionary advantage.

What are the advantages of flightlessness?

The advantages of flightnessess depend on the environment in which a particular bird lives. Flightless species fall into several categories: some are large, terrestrial birds such as the ostrich, for which sheer size is a sufficient deterrent to most land-based predators. If these birds had retained the power of flight, they would never have been able to evolve to such gargantuan proportions (the ostrich is about 10 times the weight of the largest flying birds). Flightless species also thrive in aquatic environments, especially the ocean: in the case of penguins, modified wings have become flippers, enabling them to dive to great depths.

What are the disadvantages of flightlessness?

Today, the most serious disadvantage is not being able to fly away from trouble! But this was not a problem until human beings began to explore the world. Many flightless species arose on oceanic islands, where a dearth of predators made flying unnecessary. As soon as people arrived, however, the chances of survival for flightless birds dropped dramatically. This was partly because they were easy to catch for food, and partly because humans introduced predators such as rats, cats and dogs, which found them easy prey. Two of the best-known examples of flightless birds that were casualties of human expansion are the great auk and that proverbial icon of extinction, the dodo.

Did flightless birds have flightless ancestors?

Odd as it may seem, all flightless birds evolved from flying ancestors. They did so through a process known as "neoteny," or arrested development, in which characteristics normally found in the embryonic state of a bird persist into adult life. Thus all flightless birds have wings of some sort, however vestigial they may appear. And these wings still have a job to do: in some cases they have evolved into very different structures, such as the flippers of penguins, which propel them through the water; in others, including the ostrich, they are used in courtship display.

What proportion of the world's birds is flightless?

Fewer than 50 species, or around 0.5 percent. Many other flightless species, however, have become extinct due to the invasion of their environment by pests such as cats and rats. Errol Fuller (author of *Extinct Birds*) considers that up to one-quarter of the 80 or so species to have become extinct since 1600 were flightless. These include several species of rail confined to oceanic islands, and massive flightless giants such as the moas of New Zealand and the aepyornis, or elephant bird, of Madagascar.

Mile-high club

The highest flying bird was a Rüppell's griffon vulture, which was sucked into a jet engine over the Ivory Coast in West Africa, at an altitude of more than 36,700 feet (11,186 m) in November 1973. The greatest height at which living birds have actually been observed was roughly 30,500 feet (9,296 m): a flock of bar-headed geese flying over Mount Everest.

Does flightlessness run in families?

Yes, with a few exceptions. The best-known family of flightless birds is the penguins, all of whose 17 species are flightless — though if you see a penguin swimming underwater you might argue that it has not lost the power of flight, but simply adapted it to a different medium! The other group whose members are all flightless is the 10 or so species of ratite (ostrich, emu, rheas, cassowaries and kiwis). Flightlessness is also prevalent among rails: almost one in four living or recently extinct species are, or were, flightless. Other groups with flightless members include the grebes, cormorants, ducks, parrots and the unique kagu of New Caledonia — a peculiar species distantly related to the rails. The only passerine that has ever been described as flightless (and even then, it may have retained limited powers of flight) was the now-extinct Stephens Island wren all known specimens of which were discovered (and unfortunately killed) by the lighthouse-keeper's cat.

IN THE WATER

What proportion of the world's bird species regularly swim?

Of the world's 9,800 or so species of bird, only about 400 (about 4 percent) habitually swim on or dive under water. Those that do are mostly found in particular groups: loons, grebes, tubenoses (albatrosses, shearwaters and petrels), pelicans, cormorants, water-fowl (ducks, geese and swans), coots and gallinules, phalaropes, gulls and terns, and alcids. Several other groups, such as herons and egrets, flamingos and shorebirds, can also be classified as "waterbirds," and these include some species that do occasionally swim for short periods.

How have swimming birds adapted to an aquatic existence?

In several ingenious ways. For example, many have webbed feet to increase propulsion when swimming or diving. Ducks have fully webbed feet, while other groups such as grebes and phalaropes have either partial webs or lobes on the sides of the toes. Water is a harder medium than air through which to make headway, so some aquatic species such as penguins have developed much tighter feather patterns to create a more streamlined profile, making their plumage look more like mammalian fur than feathers. Penguins also have dense bones, unlike other birds whose bones are mostly hollow and filled with air, helping them to submerge and dive more easily.

Why don't waterbirds become waterlogged?

Many birds that habitually swim or dive have specially adapted oil glands at the base of their tail, from which they secrete an oily sub-stance that they use to waterproof their feathers. These glands are particularly well-developed in groups that spend much of their time in the water, such as penguins, ducks and gulls. A few waterbirds, how-ever, such as the frigatebirds have very small oil glands and so cannot coat their plumage adequately. These birds avoid landing on the sea because otherwise they would rapidly become waterlogged and drown.

Do all birds dive in the same way?

No. Most, including penguins, loons, grebes, cormorants, alcids and several species of duck, dive from the surface of the water. Some of

The American dipper is a delightful little bird that openly hunts for food along and in rocky streams and rivers of western North America. It is the only representative of the family Cinclidae on the continent.

these, such as penguins and alcids, propel themselves using their wings; others, like loons, grebes and ducks, use their powerful webbed or lobed feet. A few birds, including gannets, boobies, terns, kingfishers and fish-eating raptors, dive into the water from the air. Some, for example, the gannet, plunge in deeply; others, such as fish eagles, prefer to snatch prey from the surface.

Are there any aquatic songbirds?

Yes: the five members of the dipper family. These extraordinary little birds have adapted to feed underwater and even walk along the bottom of streams and rivers — a skill shared by very few other warm-blooded creatures except the hippopotamus! Dippers' adaptations include dense plumage, flaps over their nostrils and a specially adapted transparent eyelid enabling them to see their prey while keeping the water out.

ON LAND

How do birds get about on land?

Some run or walk. Others hop, using both legs together in a single motion. By and large, nonpasserines do the former, while — with a few exceptions, including crows, starlings, pipits and wagtails — passerines do the latter.

Which birds move best on the ground?

Many aquatic birds such as grebes and divers are pretty useless on terra firma. Aerial species such as albatrosses, shearwaters and many birds of prey tend to move very clumsily. Some species, however, have become expert runners. These include the larger ratites (e.g., ostrich, rheas), game birds such as partridges, shore birds like the sanderling, and of course the two species whose name celebrates their prowess: the roadrunners!

Which birds are the least capable of walking?

Swifts and hummingbirds, whose legs and feet are very small indeed, are almost helpless on the ground. In fact most swifts can do no more than cling to vertical surfaces with their forward-pointing toes (the name of their order, Apodiformes, means "lacking feet"). Also, loons and grebes have legs set so far back on their body that they have trouble propelling themselves while on land. For swifts and hummingbirds the inability to walk is the trade-off for an essentially aerial existence; for divers and grebes it is the trade-off for an aquatic one.

Flipper power

The world's fastest swimming birds are penguins, which can swim at speeds of about 9.3 miles per hour (15 km/h) in pursuit of their prey. Gentoo penguins have been timed at over 22 miles per hour (35 km/h) over short bursts — roughly five times as fast as an Olympic freestyle champion. Penguins are also undoubtedly the most aquatic birds. Some penguin species may spend as much as three-quarters of their daily lives in the water, and outside the breeding season will stay away from land completely for several months at a time.

How do woodpeckers climb trees?

Woodpeckers (and other arboreal groups such as creepers and nuthatches) have special adaptations for climbing up the trunks and branches of trees. In the case of woodpeckers, most species have two toes pointed forward and two pointing back, enabling them to grip the surface of bark. Woodpeckers also have a stiff tail, which they use as a prop to stabilize themselves — an adaptation shared by birds such as the brown creeper, which also has long claws for clinging to bark.

How do nuthatches climb down trees?

The world's 25 or so species of nuthatch share one characteristic unique among birds: the ability to climb down trees headfirst, as well as up. This is despite the fact that they lack the stiff tail of woodpeckers and creepers. Instead, their ability derives from the way they place their feet when climbing — one foot above, the other below — enabling them to move up, across or down the surface of a tree.

ALL TOGETHER

Why do birds form flocks?

For a number of reasons, of which the most important are finding food, avoiding attack by predators and migrating. In every case the primary motivation comes from the individual, for whom the advantages of joining a group outweigh those of remaining solitary.

How does flocking help a bird find food?

Once one bird has discovered a good food source, another will soon spot it and join in. As the gathering attracts other passing birds, a flock may form. This behavior is especially useful for species whose food tends to be scattered or concentrated in a small area, such as seabirds in the open ocean or vultures on the African savannah. As a

The white-breasted nuthatch, like other nuthatches, typically moves down tree trunks headfirst. This species and the similar red-breasted nuthatch share much of the same range, but experienced birders can tell the two species apart by the sounds they make.

result, both seabirds and vultures are particularly adept at noticing concentrations of their fellow birds from a distance. For some birds, flocking can help concentrate their food source: pelicans work together to corral fish into shallow water, where they can all feed more easily.

Plumbing the depths

The deepest diving bird is the emperor penguin, which has been reliably recorded at a depth of 875 feet (267 m), though a depth of more than 1,650 feet (503 m) has been reported. Its smaller relative the king penguin has been recorded at depths of 790 feet (241 m). Among flying birds, both common and Brünnich's murres have been recorded at depths of up to 660 feet (201 m). The longest time a bird can stay underwater is about 18 minutes, a record also held by the emperor penguin. Cetaceans, however, can easily outdo any bird when it comes to diving: sperm whales have been recorded 1.6 miles (2.8 km) below the surface and can stay underwater for over an hour.

How does flocking help a bird avoid being attacked?

The other main advantage of flocking — either while feeding, migrating or going to roost (see page 100) — is that it reduces an individual's chances of being attacked and killed by a predator. This comes down to basic mathematics: the more individuals there are for a predator to attack, the less chance a single bird has of falling victim. Another advantage is that a flock provides numerous eyes and ears to look and listen out for predators, and if one does appear, individuals can join together to mob it. Finally, rapid twisting and turning movements by flocks such as shorebirds or starlings are thought to confuse an attacking predator.

How does flocking help during migration?

Flocking is also advantageous for some, though not all, migrating birds, notably those that travel in flocks made up of family groups, such as geese and cranes. There are two main advantages. First, by flying in a V-formation they reduce wind resistance, with birds taking turns in the lead position (rather like a team of racing cyclists). Second, traveling together reduces the chances of getting lost, especially for young birds on their first migratory journey. Having said that, many birds (especially songbirds) migrate either in loose flocks or on their own and still manage to reach their destination.

How do birds in a flock communicate?

Generally by call — as in the "contact calls" made by wood-warblers when on migration or the flight calls of shorebirds. If a predator should approach, the first individual to spot it will often sound the alarm, warning other flock members of the danger and enabling the alert individual to escape in the resulting confusion.

Why don't birds in a flock collide with each other?

Fast-moving flocks operate on the principle that each individual bird is able to maintain its own "personal space" — in effect a mini-territory that no other bird may enter. Flocking birds have an instinctive appreciation of the distance they must maintain from the bird in front and those on each side, even when moving at high speed, and the ability to take evasive action if these birds deviate from their course or slow down. This produces the twisting and turning effect seen in vast flocks of ducks or shorebirds, in which the flock appears to behave virtually as a single organism.

So how do the birds in a large flock all turn at the same time?

By a process similar to that of "the wave" sports fans perform in a stadium, in which as one bird on the edge of the flock begins to turn, the bird next to it turns a split second later, and so on. Birds have a lightning-fast reaction time and can see an approaching movement, enabling them to anticipate it. As a result a wave can move through a flock in less than 15 milliseconds — to our eyes appearing almost instantaneous.

Are flocks always made up of a single species?

No — mixed flocks frequently occur. These usually comprise several closely related species, such as ducks, shorebirds, thrushes or finches, but sometimes also include totally unrelated groups, such as winter flocks in woodlands that may contain chickadees, nuthatches, creepers and even the occasional woodpecker. Again, the advantages of flocking and the shared goal (e.g., finding food) outweigh any disadvantages such as competition.

Do all birds flock?

No. Some, such as cuckoos, are almost always solitary, whether feeding or on migration. Most birds of prey and owls are usually found singly or in pairs, though there are exceptions, including some small falcons that feed in loose flocks. Other raptors that are usually solitary will migrate in flocks.

What is "mobbing"?

The attacking and harassment of a predator by a group of smaller birds, usually songbirds. This normally takes place when a predator such as a hawk or owl turns up unexpectedly in the birds' territory, or they discover it while out feeding. If the predator is flying, several birds may fly up to hassle it until it departs; if it is perched, they will fly down and attack it, calling noisily until it has had enough and flies off. Some mobbing birds are little smaller than the object of their fury: crows, for instance, often mob larger raptors. Other kinds of predator may also provoke an attack, and birdwatchers searching for owls in the tropics should bear in mind that small birds often mob snakes!

Does mobbing work?

In most cases, effective mobbing will drive away a bird of prey, at least temporarily. If a bird gets too close, though, it may fall victim to the very danger it was trying to prevent! Occasionally, a bird that closely resembles a predator, such as a passing heron, will be mobbed in error. On the other hand a predator that is a familiar part of the scenery, such as a breeding peregrine, will often be left in peace and mobbed only if it actually tries to attack another bird.

What is "roosting"?

Basically, taking a rest. Although this term is often used to describe large nocturnal gatherings of sleeping birds, it can also apply to just a single bird, can take place at any time of day or night and is not necessarily a prelude to sleep.

Do birds always roost at night?

Certainly not. Nocturnal species such as owls roost by day, when they may sometimes be seen perched in a hole or crevice in a tree. Shorebirds may roost by day or night: their feeding times are governed by the twice daily rise and fall of the tide, rather than by the circadian rhythm that rules most other birds' lives.

Why do birds roost together?

Mainly to avoid attack by predators, just as flocking enables each individual to reduce its chances of being attacked. Roosting birds benefit from the rule of "safety in numbers" by remaining collectively alert, and can respond quickly to alarm calls. Roosting close to other birds can also be a good way to keep warm.

Sprint finish

On the ground, the world's fastest running bird is the ostrich, which typically runs at a speed of about 28 to 39 miles per hour (45–63 km/h) and can reach speeds of more than 44 miles per hour (71 km/h) over short distances — faster than most birds can fly! The fastest mammal, the cheetah, can sprint at more than 62 miles per hour (100 km/h) over short distances. The fastest runner among flying birds is the greater roadrunner, which far prefers running to flying and can reach speeds of up to 25 miles per hour (40 km/h).

Does roosting have any disadvantages?

Not many for the birds, though overcrowding may increase the risk of spreading disease. Bird roosts, however, can cause all sorts of problems for people: large gatherings of pigeons or starlings befoul building ledges with their droppings, which may carry dangerous diseases, and noise from bird roosts can be a problem in residential areas.

6 WHAT DO BIRDS EAT?

FEEDING

EATING

What do birds eat?

A better question might be, what don't birds eat? Hardly an edible item exists that doesn't pass down some avian gullet. Typical diets include insects (e.g., warblers and flycatchers), seeds (finches and buntings), meat (birds of prey and owls), fish (seabirds and herons), fruit (parrots and turacos), aquatic invertebrates and plants (ducks and geese), grain (gamebirds) and crustaceans (shorebirds, gulls and seabirds). For the more sophisticated palate, there is also nectar (hummingbirds), lichens (ptarmigan), tree sap (sapsuckers), rotting meat (vultures), wax (honeyguides) and even feces (gulls, crows and vultures). If it is edible (and sometimes even if isn't), some bird somewhere will eat it.

How often do birds eat?

Feeding rates vary dramatically, from once every second or two (insect-eating songbirds) to just once a day (several species of grouse). Large birds of prey such as vultures will gorge themselves on a carcass and not feed again for several days afterward.

How much do birds eat?

This depends on the size of the bird. In general, the smaller and lighter a bird, the more it will eat in proportion to its body weight. Large birds such as raptors tend to eat about one-quarter of their body weight a day, while smaller birds such as tits and warblers may eat up to one-half — though in actual terms this may be only a few grams. The heartiest eaters are the tiny hummingbirds, some of which consume more than twice their weight every day — mostly in the form of nectar. The amount birds eat changes from season to season too: small birds must eat more in cold weather to maintain their body heat, or they risk death. Long-distance migrants also feed much more intensely just before setting off, to build up fat reserves for the journey ahead.

Where do birds find their food?

The surface of our planet is one big buffet for birds. Some feed on the ground (e.g., robins, thrushes and pigeons); others do so in trees (warblers, tits and parrots). Some catch their prey on the wing (swallows, swifts and falcons); others probe into the mud (shore-birds). Some forage beneath tree bark (woodpeckers, creepers and nuthatches), while others dive beneath the surface of a river, lake or ocean (dippers, ducks and gannets). If there is an ecological niche with food on offer, at least one species of bird has evolved to exploit it.

How do birds find their food?

Each has its own strategies, according to what it feeds on. Many birds simply forage around their chosen habitat, picking up morsels as they go. Others must hunt more actively, as in the case of a swallow snapping up tiny airborne insects or an eagle chasing and catching a hare. In some places, such as the tree canopy of a rainforest, food is everywhere. In others, such as the open ocean, food may be concentrated in one particular place and take time and effort to find. Some birds, such as woodland passerines or farmland species, usually feed within a relatively small area, while others, such as seabirds and large raptors, may have to wander for hundreds of miles to find a meal. Many species, including New and Old World vultures, corvids and gulls, scavenge for dead or dying creatures, but in recent years they have also become adept at exploiting human-made food sources such as garbage dumps.

Which senses help birds find food?

Mainly eyesight — used either to spot food or watch the actions of their fellow birds, following them to it. Some species, however, such as nocturnal owls and nightjars, hunt mainly by hearing, while a few, including turkey vultures and storm-petrels, do so by smell. Turkey vultures and their relatives have "see-through" nostrils that improve the flow of air through their nasal cavity and enable them to pinpoint the source of rotting food odors very effectively. Finally, some birds that probe deep into the mud or earth, such as the snipe and the woodcock, find their prey by touch, using sensitive nerve endings at the tip of their bill.

Do birds chew their food?

No. Birds lack teeth (which would make them too heavy to fly), so they swallow their food whole. Some birds of prey tear their meat into chunks and strips to make this job easier, and seed-eating birds such as finches normally crush a seed in their bill and discard the shell and husk before swallowing it.

How do birds digest their food?

After birds swallow food, it passes down the esophagus, either into the "crop" (a storage area in the throat) or directly into the first section of the bird's stomach, where digestive juices begin to dissolve it. Afterward the food passes into the second section, known as the gizzard, whose powerful muscular walls grind hard substances — effectively doing the same job as a mammal's teeth. Some food items such as fur and bones are impossible to digest and are regurgitated as a "pellet." Owls are particularly well-known for their pellets, which can often be found beneath trees at regular roosting sites.

Do all birds have a "crop"?

No, most do not. Those that do include pigeons and doves, parrots and gamebirds, and it allows them to store items for later consumption (when there is a sudden glut of food) or to bring food back to the nest and regurgitate it to feed their young. Storing food in this way also enables a bird to feed quickly, minimizing the risk of attack.

Empty freezer

The longest a bird can go without food is almost four months, in the case of the male emperor penguin, which is left incubating his solitary egg while his partner travels hundreds of miles to the open ocean to find food. During this time, he lives on his considerable fat reserves. Even after his mate returns, he still has to make the long walk back to the ocean to feed himself.

Why do some birds eat grit or lick salt?

Many birds eat small items of grit to improve the grinding process of their gizzard. This habit is particularly common among seed-eating birds such as pigeons and doves, finches and buntings, gamebirds and ostriches. Salt licking, best known among certain species of parrot, may be a way of neutralizing toxic substances in their food.

How do birds excrete?

Unlike us mammals, birds have only a single opening for excretion, the cloaca, which also has to handle reproduction and egg-laying. Before excretion, most of the liquid waste is reabsorbed into the body, so birds' waste products are generally fairly solid.

Do birds cooperate to find food?

Some certainly do, either intentionally or unintentionally. Waterbirds such as pelicans and cormorants, and some ducks including the Northern shoveler, will congregate in a suitable area and surround their prey, herding it into one concentrated mass and feeding from it. Some woodland species may also cooperate, such as mixed flocks of tits, which call constantly to each other (though this may simply be to keep the flock together as a safety measure).

How do young birds learn to find food?

Like young animals of all kinds, including human babies, birds learn to find food by a combination of instinct, observation and of course trial and error. The pecking instinct is innate, as can be seen in newly hatched chickens or gamebirds. As it grows, a young bird learns by observing the feeding actions of its parents and other birds in the group, and can soon distinguish between tasty and toxic. Some adult raptors, such as peregrines, will actively help their offspring catch food by driving prey toward them.

Sugar rush

The birds that eat the most food (relative to their body weight) are undoubtedly the hummingbirds, which will consume about twice their body weight every day, mainly in the form of nectar (though also including some tiny insects).

How have birds' bills adapted to their different diets?

Because most birds find food using their bill, this appendage has evolved into a wonderful variety of shapes and sizes to exploit the full spectrum of grub on offer. Waders serve as an example: semipalmated plovers have a short, stubby bill for picking up small items; dunlins have a longer, thinner, slightly decurved bill for probing beneath the surface; avocets have an upcurved bill for sweeping across the water to snap up tiny morsels; and snipe have a long, thick bill for poking right down into the mud. For every wader species, a bill has evolved that is shaped to deal with the particular food it eats (and in doing so, has provided birders with a good way to tell them all apart). Other amazing bills include those of hummingbirds, which are long and thin for probing flowers for nectar; flamingos, whose

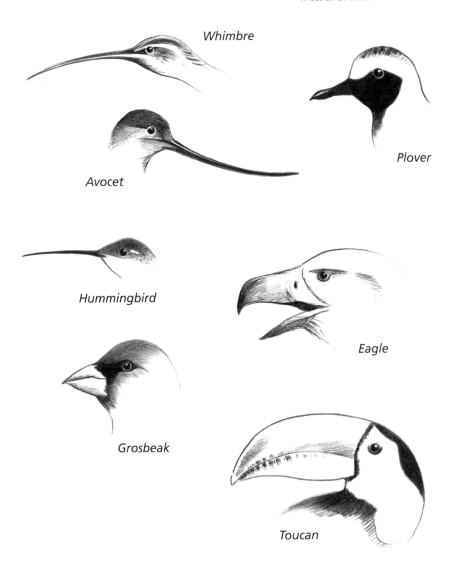

The bills of different bird species vary enormously in size and shape to suit their particular feeding habits.

bills are shaped to allow them to filter out tiny organisms using their tongue as a pump; and birds of prey, whose bills are hooked and powerful for tearing meat.

Do pelicans really keep food in their large beaks?

"A wonderful bird is the pelican; his beak will hold more than his belly can ..." This famous rhyme alludes to the extensible throat pouch, called a gular sac, that hangs below a pelican's beak and is used to "net" fish rather than store them. The pelican first swallows any fish it catches and then either digests it or regurgitates it later to feed its young.

Do all birds have a specialized diet?

No. Some groups, such as many gulls and crows, will consume most edible items they come across; other species are best equipped for dealing with one particular kind of food, as is the case with hummingbirds (nectar), raptors (meat) and seabirds (fish). Some species are even more specialized: the snail kite of the Americas, as its name suggests, feeds almost exclusively on aquatic snails, though even this species will take other kinds of food when conditions force it to. Specialization is a good way to avoid competition and works well in times of plenty; but it does make the species vulnerable to any environmental changes that threaten its favored food supply.

Do birds change their diet from season to season?

Many have to, since some foods are simply not available all year round. Migrants also change their diet, stocking up on berries in autumn to provide energy for the long journey south. Many birds can also broaden their diet to take advantage of brief seasonal bonanzas: tawny eagles, for example, will ignore other foods to binge on termites when these flying insects emerge onto the African savannah in their periodic millions.

Why don't birds eat leaves?

Unlike ruminant mammals such as cattle, deer and antelopes, birds are unable to digest leaves. Also, the nutritional value of leaves is very low, so a huge volume must be consumed to derive enough energy to make eating leaves worthwhile. For flying birds, this would seriously affect their ability to take to the air. One species, however, the hoatzin of the Amazon rainforest, does eat leaves as part of its diet. It is able to do so because, unlike other vegetarian birds that break up food in the gizzard, the hoatzin has a crop with thick, muscular walls and a horny lining. This enables it to crush the leaves before they are finally digested in the stomach. As a result the hoatzin often appears "front-heavy," especially after a large meal, and can keep its balance when its crop is full only by resting on its specially developed breastbone.

Do birds eat other birds?

Yes. Apart from the obvious examples (day-flying birds of prey such as eagles, hawks and falcons), other bird-eating groups include owls, shrikes, and some storks and herons. Some birds of prey will feed on other raptors: the European eagle owl, for example, frequently takes buzzards and sometimes even long-eared owls. Larger tubenoses such as the southern giant petrel prey on penguin chicks — a behavior featured in the movie *March of the Penguins.*

What proportion of birds are predators?

That depends on how you define the word "predator." If we count only birds that feed mostly on warm-blooded creatures (i.e, other birds and mammals), the term would include only diurnal raptors (such as eagles, hawks and falcons), owls and shrikes. These groups contain roughly 600 species in all (or around 6 percent of the world's birds). If fish-eating birds such as the osprey, wildfowl, seabirds, herons and kingfishers are included, however, this total would rise to more than 1,000 species (over 10 percent of the world's birds). And if catching and eating any animal prey counts as being a predator, then all insect-eating birds, such as flycatchers, warblers and robins, should also count!

Are all raptors carnivorous?

No, though the vast majority are. Notable exceptions include the honey buzzard, which feeds mainly on the larvae of insects such as bees and wasps; the red-footed falcon, which eats flying insects such as locusts; and the palm-nut vulture of Africa, which, as its name suggests, feeds mainly on the fruit of the oil palm. These species, however, reflect their ancestral lineage by possessing all of the attributes we associate with birds of prey, such as a hooked bill, sharp talons and forward-facing eyes.

How do raptors catch their prey?

Mostly with their feet, grabbing or striking their target with powerful, sharp talons and squeezing or tearing it to death. Even when catching flying insects such as dragonflies, falcons like the merlin will grab them with their feet before passing them into their mouth with a single, smooth action. If feet do not finish the job, raptors will use their sharp beak to tear their victim's flesh. Falcons have a special notch in the upper mandible of their bill, called the "tomial tooth," which is adapted for severing tiny vertebrae.

Do other birds use their feet to find food?

Yes, in various different ways. Herons and egrets "foot-paddle," stirring up the mud at the bottom of the water to bring food items such as small invertebrates and plant material to the surface. Other birds, such as gulls, do a similar thing by stamping their feet repeatedly on the surface of a grassy field — an action that appears to make worms and other creatures rise to the surface. The secretary bird, a bizarre bird of prey found on the African savannah, actually stamps on its prey — a very effective way of killing beetles, rodents, lizards and even ground-dwelling birds. One species of rail, the purple swamphen of southern Europe, Africa, Asia and Australia, grips aquatic vegetation in its foot and transfers it to its mouth as if using a hand, and parrots perform a similar action when feeding on fruit.

Do birds hide or store food?

Yes, in a habit known as "caching." In times of plenty, especially in early autumn when trees are fruiting, several species will hide food in a "cache" for the coming winter. This is common among members of the crow family, such as nutcrackers and jays, which bury acorns and other seeds under leaf litter. Their ability to find this food again after months have passed may show either intuition or intelligence, but certainly demonstrates an impressive memory! Another species that regularly stores the fruit of the oak tree is the aptly-named acorn woodpecker. Found in the western United States and Mexico, this attractive woodpecker drills long rows of holes in the trunks and branches of trees, and crams an individual acorn into each one. Certain shrikes use a rather more grisly "larder" to store their food. They impale their bird, amphibian and reptile prey on the spikes of thorn bushes, a behavior that has earned them the nickname "butcher-bird."

Do birds use other animals to help them find food?

Yes, in a process known as "commensalism," defined as two species of plant or animal living closely alongside each other without becoming interdependent. Thus European robins will follow wild boars and pick

Big game hunters

The dubious honor of largest prey killed by a bird goes (posthumously) to various monkeys and small antelopes, all of which regularly fall victim to some of the larger eagles. The crowned eagle of sub-Saharan Africa has even been known to kill a subadult impala weighing 66 pounds (29.94 kg) — five times heavier than the bird itself. While these formidable predators are fully capable of killing animals larger than themselves, however, they cannot carry away anything that weighs more than they do. The largest wild animal known to have been killed and carried away by a bird is a 15-pound (6.8 kg) male red howler monkey killed by a harpy eagle in Manu National Park, Peru, in 1990. This feat is all the more amazing given that the eagle itself would have weighed no more than 20 pounds (9.07 kg).

up worms and other food items that they dig up while foraging. In recent times robins have taken to following human gardeners for the same reason! Cattle egrets and several species of gull and wader will follow large domestic mammals such as cows and horses, or wild

The cattle egret, a native of the Old World, arrived in South America sometime near the end of the 19th century and spread north from there. This species often feeds on insects that cattle disturb as they graze.

mammals such as elephants and wildebeest, to take advantage of the insects they either disturb or attract. Some species, such as oxpeckers, ride almost permanently on the backs of large mammals, feeding on the insects attracted by the animal's body heat and sweat and even using its hair as nesting material! But perhaps the most extraordinary example is that of the antbirds, a South American family of passerines. Antbirds do not feed on ants, as might be expected from their name; instead, several species have learned to follow troops of giant army ants as they sweep across the ground, snapping up any insects they flush along the way.

Do any birds have symbiotic relationships with other creatures?

Symbiosis, defined as a relationship between two different species that brings mutual benefit to both, is extremely rare in birds. The best-known example is the honeyguides, an African and Asian family related to the woodpeckers, whose family name, Indicatoridae, gives a clue to their unique skill. Two species of honeyguide are especially partial to honeycomb and beeswax but are unable to obtain these foods without help, as they would be attacked by the bees. So they have learned to guide, using their call, a honey-loving mammal, the ratel, or honey-badger, to the bees' nest. The badger is immune to bee stings and rips out the nest, allowing the bird to feast on the remaining comb. Human observers have also learned to follow the honeyguide, which has thus developed a symbiotic relationship with man in some places. Local custom ensures that people always reward the bird by leaving it a portion — otherwise next time it might take its revenge by leading them to a venomous snake. It might also be argued that garden birds coming to feeding stations have developed a similar relationship: we give them food; they give us pleasure!

Man-eater!

There is no shortage of lurid tales that describe immense eagles, especially golden eagles, snatching up small children. Such horrors can generally be dismissed as the stuff of myth and legend. A handful of more recent records concerning the crowned eagle, however, if genuine make it possibly the only bird to prey on human beings. These records, which must represent extremely unusual circumstances, include the discovery of part of a child's skull in a crowned eagle's nest. Since this species never preys on carrion and often takes monkeys at least as large as a human baby, the unfortunate infant was almost certainly snatched while still alive.

Do some birds steal from others?

Yes. This process is known as "kleptoparasitism" — or simply as "piracy" by nonscientists. Many birds will opportunistically snatch food from another — just watch the thieving at a gull colony. But two groups of seabirds have turned a life of crime into a fine art. Skuas, jaegers and frigatebirds are the pirates of the air, pursuing and harassing other birds until they drop their food, then catching it acrobatically in midair. Skuas' and jaegers' victims include terns and gulls, while frigatebirds often pursue elegant tropic birds in a real "beauty and the beast" contest. Large raptors such as the bald eagle also sometimes try piracy, their victim of choice often being the unfortunate osprey.

Cache prizes

Clark's nutcracker of North America is perhaps the greatest hoarder of any bird. It has been known to bury over 30,000 pine kernels in an area covering more than 200 square miles (518 km²). Even more remarkably, over the following eight months it will retrieve over 90 percent of them, even when they are hidden under a layer of snow!

Are any birds true parasites?

True parasitism — defined as the one-way exploitation of one living organism (the host) by another (the parasite) — is very rare among birds. Parasitic birds include the sharp-beaked ground-finch (or vampire finch) of the Galápagos, which regularly takes blood from the base of the feathers of masked and red-footed boobies, and the kelp gull, which has been known to peck at sores on the backs of southern right whales and eat the flesh.

What is a "scavenger"?

Any species that feeds primarily on dead meat, such as marabou storks and both New and Old World vultures. Despite being unrelated, these latter two families have evolved a very similar build and appearance, including having bare heads that, if covered with feathers, would become clogged with blood and gore. Other species, such as magpies and crows, have a more varied diet but will feed on a carcass when opportunity presents one. Most gruesome of all, turnstones have been recorded feeding on a human corpse washed up on the tideline.

How do vultures avoid food poisoning?

By having very strong stomachs! Vultures have a highly specialized digestive system, containing powerful acids to neutralize even the most putrescent meat that would quickly kill a human being.

DRINKING

How do birds drink?

Most birds have to tip their heads back to allow water to run down their throat, as they lack the ability to swallow. A few groups of birds, though, including pigeons and doves, the African mousebirds and some species of finch, are able to drink without lifting their heads, using their tongue to create a sucking action. Other species such as swallows and martins fly low over water, dipping their bill just below the surface to grab a beakfull of liquid as they pass. In the Antarctic, penguins will drink by eating snow.

Where do birds find water to drink?

In all kinds of places, some obvious, such as lakes, puddles and ponds, and others less so, such as dew, or rainwater on leaves or in the base of plants. Some species drink falling rain directly. But many, especially insect-eaters, get most of the liquid they need from their food.

Going large

The biggest food item eaten by any land bird must surely be a dead African elephant, which may draw hundreds of vultures of various species to binge on its bloated carcass. But this is a mere snack beside the beached whales on which scavenging seabirds such as the southern giant petrel and Antarctic skua gorge themselves whenever they get the opportunity.

How often do birds need to drink?

This varies considerably, depending on their diet. Insect-eating birds such as warblers may need to drink only once a day, whereas birds that feed on seeds and other dry foods will have to do so at least two or three times. Birds that obtain all their liquid requirements from their food do not have to drink at all.

How do young birds in the nest get water?

Usually their parents carry water in their bill and then pass it drop by drop into the mouths of the nestlings. The desert-dwelling sand-grouse, however, has evolved a unique way of carrying back more water in very dry conditions: the male soaks his breast in water and then flies back to the nest where the thirsty young are able to get moisture from his uniquely adapted, spongelike feathers.

How do seabirds drink salt water without being harmed?

Although most birds cannot drink salt water, oceangoing seabirds such as albatrosses and shearwaters have a specially adapted salt gland in their nasal region, which enables them to excrete the high levels of salt found in seawater through special tubes on their nose — an adaptation that gives them the collective name "tubenoses." As a result they can stay out on the open ocean for weeks, months or even years.

BACKYARD BIRDS

Is it good to feed backyard birds?

In general, yes. Feeding prolongs the lives of individual birds and helps maintain numbers. Without supplementary food, many birds would die, especially during bad winter weather. With so much damage and destruction elsewhere, backyards and gardens have now become one of the most important habitats for many species — especially songbirds. Feeding birds also brings us less tangible benefits: millions of people enjoy the hobby, and it leads many on to a more active interest such as birding or conservation.

Bird nuts!

The champion bird-feeding nation is, not surprisingly, the United States, whose bird-lovers spend approximately $2.2 billion per year on bird food — roughly the same as the gross domestic product of Nicaragua!

Can feeding birds do any harm?

Possibly, yes. Concentrating birds in one area can help spread diseases. Also, it may tip the balance in favor of predators such as hawks or cats by concentrating birds in one area, where the attacker can claim a "free lunch." A more subtle argument against feeding is that by artificially helping birds we are acting against nature, and supporting individuals that otherwise would have died. As a result, it is argued, the population as a whole becomes less "healthy." It might also be argued, however, that we have destroyed so much natural habitat that we have a moral duty to lend the birds a helping hand. Overall, the benefits of feeding appear to outweigh the drawbacks.

What are the best types of food to give birds?

Birds feed to gain energy, so the best foods are those that deliver the purest form of energy in the shortest time. For this reason, sunflower seeds are better than peanuts; shelled "sunflower hearts" are best of all, as the bird does not need to spend valuable time removing the kernel from the husk. Fat, in the form of fat balls or suet, is another high-energy food and is especially valuable in winter. Live food such as mealworms can also be a vital supplement during the breeding season, when nestlings and parent birds need all the help they can get.

Should I feed birds all year round?

Yes, definitely. Despite the long-held belief that we should feed birds only during winter, scientists have now proved that feeding brings benefits to birds all year round. The most important times of year to feed are spring (when parent birds must lay eggs and feed young) and during any prolonged period of harsh winter weather.

How else can I attract birds to my backyard?

There are four other areas to focus on if you wish to attract more birds — and a greater variety of species — to your backyard. First, provide water as well as food; water is essential to birds for drinking and bathing. A birdbath is great, and a pond is even better. Second, provide a place for birds to nest, either in the form of suitable shrubs and bushes or by putting up nestboxes. Third, guard against pests by keeping your feeding station clean and tidy, and against predators, especially cats, by making them unwelcome! Finally, growing a selection of native plants — including flowering annuals, bushes and shrubs, and trees — will provide natural food in the form of nectar, berries, fruit and insects for the birds to eat.

How else do birds take advantage of humans for food?

Apart from the vast amount we spend on deliberately providing food for birds, our modern lifestyles and wasteful habits provide unintentional rich pickings. Birds have always followed human hunters and fishers to scavenge carcasses or pick up any waste scraps; in the modern world birds have a vast range of other opportunities to take advantage of us. No landfill site (a euphemism for garbage dump) would be complete without its hordes of gulls, crows and — in tropical regions — kites and vultures, scavenging for scraps of waste food.

Grain stores are also popular among seed-eating birds, though in recent years less wasteful storage methods have reduced this food supply. Seabirds will follow fishing boats to feed on scraps and waste cast overboard, and passenger and cargo ships churn up food items from beneath the surface for birds to pick up. Even our modern transport system provides a steady supply of roadkill for enterprising species such as crows and kites.

7 WHY DO BIRDS SING?

COMMUNICATION

Why do birds sing?

For us, birdsong may be a thing of beauty, but for birds, it is all about love and war. War, because one reason birds sing is to defend their territory against a rival. Love, because the other reason is to attract a passing female and persuade her to mate.

Why do birds use sound, instead of showing off their plumage?

Lots of birds do indeed use visual signals. For example, colonial nesters such as seabirds perform elaborate displays to warn off rivals and attract a mate. But species living in woods or forests are often hidden from view, so birdsong evolved as the best way to communicate over long distances. For songbirds, sound also enables them to communicate in the period before sunrise, in the celebrated "dawn chorus." Many species, from grouse to birds-of-paradise, use both sight and sound to attract a female.

Can all birds sing?

No. Apart from the 6,000 or so species of songbird, most birds cannot sing, though this depends on how "singing" is defined. Many nonpasserines have special vocalizations in the breeding season that

The drumming of the male ruffed grouse is a common sound in deciduous and mixed forests of North America. The bird creates the sound by rapidly flapping its wings.

are quite different from their calls. For example, some shorebirds sit on an exposed perch and deliver what sounds very like a song.

What is the difference between a song and a call?

Songs are more complex series of notes or phrases, uttered almost solely by male birds, usually in spring, and used to repel rival males or attract a mate. Calls, on the other hand, are short, simple utterances, produced by both males and females throughout the year, for a variety of reasons. In addition songs are largely confined to the group of birds appropriately known as "songbirds." Generally, songs are also more attractive to the human ear than calls; thus the American robin's deep, fluty and tuneful song is justly celebrated, while its various calls are not.

Are any birds completely silent?

Although most birds have some kind of song or call, a few groups, such as New World vultures and storks, lack the vocal mechanism to make complex sounds, so apart from making the occasional hiss, grunt or croak they are usually silent. Incidentally, the name "mute swan" arose because this species does not call in flight, unlike other swans.

Do only males sing?

By and large, yes, though there are exceptions, such as North America's most abundant bird, the red-winged blackbird. Female blackbirds sing throughout the breeding season, either to communicate with their mate or, using a slightly different sound, to warn off rival females. This is vital because male blackbirds are polygynous — they will mate with several females if they get the chance! By singing the female increases her chances of keeping her mate faithful. Other North American species of which females also sing include northern cardinal, rose-breasted grosbeak and several species of thrush.

Why don't females usually sing?

Because generally they don't have to defend a territory or take the lead in courtship, though in fact the female's role in choosing a mate is much more active than we once thought. There is also a physiological explanation as to why females seldom sing: they don't usually have such high levels of testosterone, the hormone that triggers male song at the start of the breeding season.

What message does a singing bird send to his rivals?

A male singing in his territory is sending a clear message: "this is my patch, so keep out!" The louder and more frequent the song, the more likely a rival will get the message. But in species whose territories are fairly close together, such as the American robin, the male will leave distinct gaps between phrases so that he can detect any answering male in the vicinity.

Is song always an effective deterrent?

No. A rival male who does not yet have a territory of his own may enter another male's territory and begin singing himself instead of fleeing; this is a clear signal to the occupier that the newcomer poses a threat. The two rivals will then take part in a "knockout competition," in which the winner will usually be the bird with the "best" song.

Does the rivalry ever go further?

In a few cases, rival males will resort to physical violence, one bird attacking the other until either the occupier or the intruder retreats. European robins are particularly aggressive; males occasionally fight to the death.

How do male birds avoid a fight?

The occupying bird usually wants to avoid physical aggression, so he adopts a range of tactics designed to deter any possible rival. This generally involves singing as loudly and for as long as possible, sending the signal that he is not to be messed with. He will also patrol the borders of his territory, singing at several points around the boundary, often on exposed song posts where he can be easily seen. Together these strategies create the impression that the territory is larger than it actually is.

Do male birds ever change their songs?

Yes, sometimes. Males in the African family of robin-chats will change their song to outshine rival males, so that if an intruder sings the same song as the territory holder, the latter will switch to a new one. If the rival imitates the new song, the territory holder will switch songs again, and so on.

How does a male's song attract the female?

Like humans, birds attract a mate in a number of different ways, of which song is only one. By and large, the more frequent, persistent, varied and, in some cases, complex the song, the more likely a passing female is to stop and check out her potential mate.

Is a male with a "better" song more likely to attract a mate?

Yes, but this depends on what is meant by "better." Some birds, such as the red-eyed vireo, have to our ears a fairly monotonous song, which they repeat with little or no variation. Others have a more tuneful (and to our ears, attractive) song. At the greatest extreme, the northern mockingbird utters an extraordinary variety of notes and phrases, often for hours on end. But human perceptions of tunefulness or originality are irrelevant. What is important within any single species is the quality of the song, which may be measured in volume, frequency or complexity. This quality is what suggests the bird's breeding potential and is the key factor in influencing a female's choice of mate.

Once a male has attracted the female, does he stop singing?

Sometimes, yes — especially if the species is monogamous (i.e., males and females are faithful to each other throughout the breeding season). Others, especially polygynous species such as the marsh wren, of which males mate with several females, carry on singing to defend their territory against intruding males.

Why do birds sing mainly at dawn?

There are several reasons why the peak of birdsong occurs so early in the day, during what is celebrated as the "dawn chorus." First, it is still dark, so rather than waste energy on trying to find food that is difficult to see, a bird is better off marking its territory. Second, females are often at their most fertile at dawn, so the male must make a special effort to guard against a rival mating with "his" female. Finally, it is much easier to hear birdsong at dawn, not only because in our towns and cities there is less interference from traffic noise, but also because weather conditions are generally better at this time of day, with less wind and air turbulence. Another factor is "temperature inversion," in which a layer of cold air is trapped close to the ground by a warm layer above. Sounds reflect off the boundary between these layers, allowing birdsong to carry farther.

Name that tune

The widest repertoire of any bird is that of the brown thrasher of North America. This member of the mockingbird family has as many as 2,000 different songs, about 10 times the number written by the Beatles! This is far and away the largest "songbook" of any bird; challengers include the nightingale (between 100 and 300 different songs), the song thrush (between 140 and 220) and the northern mockingbird (up to 150).

Do they sing at other times of day?

Yes, some males sing at all hours — especially early in the breeding season when they have not yet attracted a mate and their territory may still be at risk from rivals. Generally, though, song activity declines during the middle of the day (especially during hot weather when singing requires more energy) and reaches a peak again in the early evening; the "dusk chorus," though, is neither as loud nor quite as intense as its dawn counterpart. At dusk a similar temperature inversion occurs as at dawn and has the same effect.

Why do some birds sing at night?

Some of the same reasons for singing at dawn apply to singing at night: it is quieter then, the air is often more still than during the day and most songbirds are unable to feed at night. Those species that do sing at night face less competition from other species: unlike at dawn, when the whole orchestra is performing at full volume, nocturnal singers are more likely to sing solo, without so many rivals. Modern technology may also have an influence on the singing behavior of birds: northern mockingbirds often sing at night in towns and cities, where they are illuminated by street lights, which may stimulate them to believe that dawn is approaching.

Do birds sing all year round?

Generally, no. In the temperate parts of North America and Europe, most birds breed during a period from February or March to June or July, roughly coinciding with the northern spring. Hence the gradual buildup of song from late winter onward, stimulated by the steady increase in the length of the days. Song reaches a peak in May when both resident and migrant birds are in full song. Nevertheless birdsong can be heard as early as November and December, especially in mild winters, or as late as August and September, toward the end of the breeding season. Some species, such as the European robin, sing throughout the autumn and winter as well. In the southern hemisphere, roughly the reverse is true, while in the tropics, the conventional four seasons do not apply, so breeding activity is either spread throughout the year or timed to coincide with periods of rainfall and the availability of food.

Do birds sing the same song all the time?

No. In general the song used to defend a territory is more direct and less complicated than that used to attract a mate. This is because the purpose of the territorial song is simple — to advertise that a particular area is already occupied — while the mating song needs a few more flourishes to persuade the female that this particular male is a "quality" bird, that is, one worth pairing up with.

How do birds sing?

Birds produce sounds through an organ in the throat called the syrinx, which is unique to birds. Air is exhaled from the lungs through the syrinx, where it passes across membranes that vibrate and produce sound. Using various pairs of muscles attached to the syrinx, the bird can then vary four different aspects of its song: pitch, tone, rhythm and volume. By doing so, birds as a whole are able to produce an incredible variety of sounds, ranging from a simple monosyllabic call to an avian aria of amazing complexity.

One-hit wonders

The title of having the smallest repertoire is shared by several bird species, including the ovenbird and white-crowned sparrow of North America, and the European redwing. These species have but a single song — though this seems no less effective at doing its job!

How do birds manage to sing continuously without appearing to take a breath?

Like human singers and musicians who play wind instruments, birds have evolved an extraordinary degree of control over their breathing, possibly by taking frequent "mini-breaths" rather than large intakes of air, which would prevent or interrupt their song. A singing canary may take up to 30 mini-breaths per second.

Can birds make different sounds at the same time?

As well as being able to vary pitch, tone, rhythm and volume, birds can produce sound simultaneously from both sides of their syrinx, which enables them effectively to combine two different sound channels into a single song. So the gray catbird is able to emit six separate sounds in half a second, three from one side of the syrinx and three from the other, which combine to create the illusion of continuous singing.

How do birds create such variety in their songs?

Most songbirds use a "kit of parts" to construct their songs. This comprises a basic template onto which they add their own variations,

Rise and shine!

Judging the best dawn chorus is obviously subjective, but it can be argued that temperate latitudes, with specific seasons and a slow, gradual sunrise, produce the best conditions for early morning song. Many would claim that if you want to hear the most intense and varied dawn chorus in the world, it is hard to beat an English woodland on a fine, still morning in May.

copying notes and phrases from their neighbors and, in some cases, mimicking other sounds they hear. Some species sing a relatively limited number of phrases, usually uttered in the same order. Others, such as the European starling, appear to have an almost limitless range of sounds, but in fact the song is made up of a series of about 20 to 60 phrases with very short gaps between them. One of the most accomplished songsters, the European nightingale, combines as many as 300 different song types in virtually random sequence — much like a jazz musician improvising on a theme.

How do birds optimize the effect of their song?

Getting your song heard by the largest number of potential rivals and mates is an important factor in breeding success, so some birds perch on top of a tree or bush, or in urban areas on the roof of a building. Where this is not possible, as in areas of open grassland, birds have found several different ways to broadcast their message more effectively, either delivering the song in a long, continuous flight or launching themselves into the air with every short burst of song.

Do birds in different habitats have different types of song?

Yes, because songs have evolved to best exploit the acoustic properties of the bird's normal surroundings. So forest-dwelling birds tend to have deep, varied, tuneful songs because high frequencies are absorbed by foliage; in open areas such as reedbeds or grasslands, more monotonous, buzzy songs tend to work better.

How do birds learn to sing?

Scientists have long debated whether birds inherit their ability to sing or learn their repertoire by imitation and practice. As with human language, the answer is that they do both. Like us, birds are born with a basic ability to vocalize but need to be exposed to full-blown song to learn it properly. So captive birds kept isolated from their fellow songsters develop a poor imitation of their "proper" song, while those exposed to the song of a different species may adapt elements of it into their own song pattern.

Do different individuals of the same species have different dialects?

Yes. For example, white-crowned sparrows from different areas of North America have quite distinctive differences in their song, and though these may be difficult for the human ear to detect, they have the effect of attracting females from only the same local area. There may be a good reason for this: a local female is more likely to be adapted to breed in local conditions than is a passing stranger. By singing in the local dialect, therefore, a male maximizes his chances of attracting a suitable mate. Eventually a particular dialect may differ so much from the original that its singers become reproductively isolated from neighboring populations and after time may even evolve into a separate species.

Can birds recognize other individuals of their own species?

Yes. It is thought that a singing male can recognize the songs of neighboring males and, as long as they stay put on their own territory, he will

Holding a tune

The record for most songs in a single day goes to the red-eyed vireo of North America. One male was apparently reported as uttering its brief song-phrase a staggering 22,197 times in 10 hours — on average once every 1.62 seconds. It is not known whether any females were impressed!

ignore them. If a stranger begins singing nearby, however, a male will go into attack mode, seeking out the intruder and chasing him away.

Do different calls have different purposes?

Calls fall into several categories. These include "contact calls," for keeping in touch with others in a feeding flock, and "alarm calls," for giving warning of an approaching predator.

Do any birds sing duets?

Some species do. This behavior is very rare among songbirds in temperate regions but is found in a variety of tropical birds. This is because in the tropics many birds maintain a year-round territory, which may be packed with breeding pairs of a wide range of species. In the resulting cacophony, a singing male cannot be sure that his mate can hear him, so singing duets evolved as a way of keeping in contact. The behavior is particularly common among African shrikes such as the tropical boubou, of which the male and female sing different "parts." Their timing is so perfect that to our ear the result often sounds like a single bird.

Do birds mimic other species?

If imitation is the sincerest form of flattery, then certain families of bird are the true sycophants of the animal kingdom. These include the starlings and mynas of Europe and Asia, the mockingbirds of the New World, the robin-chats of Africa, the lyrebirds and bowerbirds of Australasia and various species of parrot from around the world. The ability to mimic appears to have evolved simply because it may make the singer more attractive to potential mates. Poor mimics simply don't make the grade, whereas good mimics do and are able to pass on their skills to the next generation.

Can birds mimic artificial sounds?

Yes, they can do this too, despite the fact that most of these sounds are relatively new. For example, European starlings are accomplished mimics of recent technological innovations such as mobile phones and car alarms — much to the annoyance of people who would prefer a quiet life! The lyrebirds and bowerbirds of Australasia take mimicry to even greater extremes, producing convincing impressions of the clicks and whirrs of a camera's motor-drive.

Loud and proud

The award for the loudest song of any bird is shared by the four species of bellbird, from the New World cotinga family. Their calls peak at up to 100 decibels and can be heard from up to about half a mile (1 km) away. The superb lyrebird of Australia also has an extremely loud call. Neither of these birds' songs can compare with the world's loudest insect — the male cicada — which at 150 decibels is louder than a jet plane overhead!

How can birds reproduce human-like speech?

By the same process as they use to mimic other bird songs and natural sounds. Oddly, the best known imitators of human speech, the parrots, have rarely been observed mimicking it in the wild, yet in captivity one African grey parrot, named Alex, had a vocabulary of more than 800 words. Parrots have a thicker, more muscular tongue than most birds, adapted for manipulating food in the bill, which may also make them more articulate.

Do they understand what they are saying?

General opinion would claim that they don't — hence the phrase "parrot-fashion," meaning mindless imitation. Yet Alex the African grey not only was taught words but could combine them into simple

Boom boom!

The farthest carrying sound belongs to the Eurasian bittern, whose booming call can be heard up to 5 miles (8 km) away, due to its very low frequency. The kakapo, a nocturnal, flightless parrot native to New Zealand, tramples a hollow in the ground and uses this to amplify its call. By using this "booming bowl" the call can be heard at least 3.75 miles (6 km) away.

commands, and even learned to say no when refusing something he didn't want. As a result linguists are now rethinking the nature of avian mimicry.

Do birds sing in the rain?

That depends on how hard it's raining. Light rain will inhibit some birds, especially those that live in open habitats or that deliver their song from an exposed perch or in flight, but usually it won't bother birds shielded by thicker vegetation. Heavier rain, especially accompanied by strong winds, usually prevents most birds from singing; there's not much point singing in a downpour, since it would drown the singer out — in every sense.

What other sounds do birds use to communicate?

While songbirds take lead vocals, some other species are happier on percussion! The best known are woodpeckers, which drum their bills on hollow wood to defend a territory and win a mate. Other nonvocal alternatives to song include the bill-clattering used by white storks in their courtship display, and the snipe's "drumming" — a rhythmic whirring sound it makes by spreading its tail and flying very fast through the air, which vibrates through the feathers, causing the sound. In the tropics several species can produce sounds by trapping air beneath their wings and releasing it in an explosive "click." These include the white-bearded manakin of South America and various larks and cisticolas in Africa.

The oilbird, the only member of the family Steatornithidae, uses echolocation to navigate in caves. It lives in Trinidad and parts of northern South
America.

Do any birds use echolocation like bats do?

Only a select few, all of which live in caves. The South American oilbird (a relative of the nightjars) and several species of cave swiftlet
from Asia have learned to bounce their calls off solid surfaces to
locate flying prey or avoid bumping into cave walls. They are not
nearly as accomplished at this as bats, however. Echolocation in birds
is at normal frequencies, audible to the human ear, rather than at the
higher frequencies that bats use.

Cheep imitation

Picking out the world's best mimic is virtually impossible. The marsh warbler has been found to mimic the calls and songs of over 200 European and African species (the average individual can imitate 70 to 80 different species), the African grey parrot can mimic several hundred words of human speech and the superb lyrebird can imitate anything from a camera shutter to a chainsaw!

How many birds are named after their sound?

Too many to count! Some species have names that derive directly from the sound they make, including such well-known examples as the whip-poor-will and the chuck-will's-widow, two species of nightjar that are more often heard than seen. Others have names that describe their sounds, such as the trumpeter finch, screech owl or whistling duck. The best example of the latter must be the African cisticolas — a family of similar-plumaged birds whose common names reflect the importance of song in telling them apart: hence the rattling, singing, croaking, wailing, churring, tinkling, chirping, trilling, bubbling and chattering cisticolas, to name but a few. Some people even assert that the rock-loving cisticola is named not for its chosen habitat, but after its musical tastes!

Do all ducks quack?

Certainly not. The mallard, which does quack, is the world's most common and best-known species, so its call has come to represent all of its kind. But the duck family as a whole has a much broader repertoire of calls. These include a high-pitched whistle (Eurasian wigeon), a chorus of wailing cries (long-tailed duck) and a call that sounds like a respectable middle-aged woman in a state of outraged curiosity (common eider).

8 HOW DO BIRDS REPRODUCE?

BREEDING

PAIRING UP

Do all birds breed in spring?

Springtime is certainly the season of love for birds in temperate regions — "spring" being loosely defined as the period between the spring equinox and the summer solstice. In the northern hemisphere, therefore, this means a peak of breeding activity between March and June, and in the southern hemisphere between September and December. There are plenty of exceptions, even in temperate regions, where species such as the mourning dove may start breeding well before the "official" start of spring — even in November or December if the weather is particularly mild. In tropical regions, breeding is generally timed to coincide with seasonal rainfall so that there will be enough food for the young.

Why do birds breed at one particular time of year?

Birds time their breeding to coincide with the peak availability of food, which is why in Europe and North America most breed between March and July. The abundance of food at this time is especially important for species that feed on a single main type of prey, such as barn swallows (flying insects). This also suits the breeding

Young lovers/Late bloomers

The earliest age for a bird to begin breeding is between 5 and 6 weeks, in the case of several members of the quail family. The latest age for a bird to begin breeding is normally 6 to 10 years, for the larger albatrosses, and some sooty terns may not breed until they are 10 years old.

cycle of birds of prey, which make sure they have chicks in the nest when there are plenty of young songbirds to feed to them.

Why do some birds breed earlier or later than others?

Breeding outside the usual season is related to the supply of a particular food. Red crossbills start nesting in January or February so that their chicks hatch during the peak fruiting period of the spruce cones on which they feed. In contrast, Eleonora's falcon, a European bird of prey, does not breed until late summer, so it has chicks in the nest in September and October. At this time, large numbers of migrating songbirds — ideal food for the young falcons — are passing through the Mediterranean region.

How do birds know when to breed?

Birds cannot possibly know when the food supply will reach its peak. The whole process of breeding is usually governed by changes in day length. These stimulate chemicals in their brain and trigger the cycle of courtship, finding a territory and so on. Birds can be fooled by periods of very mild weather in late autumn or winter, however, which may stimulate some to begin breeding at the "wrong" time of year. Sadly this can have disastrous consequences, as a hard frost or heavy snowfall may wipe out the food supply just when the chicks need feeding.

Do all birds breed every year?

No. Although the vast majority of species, especially those in temperate regions, do breed annually, many others do not. Larger seabirds such as albatrosses have a two-year cycle, as it takes so long to raise their single huge chick that they could not possibly breed every year.

Other seabirds such as the sooty tern may breed more frequently, for example, on a nine-month cycle. And some tropical seabirds and penguins simply breed whenever it suits them, so any one colony will contain young of all ages at the same time.

At what age do birds begin to breed?

This varies considerably. In general, the longer the normal lifespan of the bird, the longer it will take to reach maturity. So most passerines breed the year after they are born, while the larger gulls take up to four years to reach maturity. At the furthest extremes, long-lived species such as albatrosses may not breed until they reach 6 or even 10 years old, while some members of the quail family have been known to breed when they are just six weeks old!

How do birds choose a mate?

The rituals of bird courtship are almost infinitely varied and complex, but the basic principle is always the same — one bird (almost always the male) tries to dazzle his way into his partner's affection by showing off. Tactics can include visual displays, as used by colorful birds such as the peacock (male Indian peafowl); vocal displays, as used by songbirds; and more complex "behavioral displays," such as the dancing of cranes or food-passing between raptors. Sometimes birds use a combination of all three tactics.

What is a "territory"?

Simply an area defended by one bird (almost always the male) to carry out the processes of breeding (courtship, copulation, nest building and raising young) without interference from rivals of the same species.

Do all birds have territories?

That depends on how the concept of "territory" is defined. Colonial species such as herons or seabirds may nest almost touching each

Many birders hope to witness the courtship dance of cranes, in which the male and female bow to each other and leap up into the air.

other but will still peck angrily at any intruder who dares to encroach on their "personal space." Species that use "leks" (see page 144) do not have territories per se but will still jostle for the best position in the lekking area to attract the most females.

Do birds defend territories outside the breeding season?

Yes, because territory is not just about breeding. Birds will also protect a food supply during the autumn and winter months, when food may be scarce. Hummingbirds may also defend a particular group of flowers against others hummingbirds to keep safe a nectar supply for themselves.

Why do birds need territories?

For many birds, especially songbirds, a territory is a vital asset in the race to reproduce. By hanging on to his own territory during the breeding season, a male can maximize his chances of attracting a mate and being able to feed his chicks. A large territory also helps him avoid being eaten: the bigger your territory, the smaller the likelihood that your particular nest will fall victim to a predator.

How big is a typical territory?

There is no such thing as a "typical" territory! A colonial nesting species such as the common murre nests within pecking distance of its rivals; large birds of prey such as golden and bald eagles may defend an area of several hundred square miles.

Home on the range

The largest bird territory, though difficult to measure, is probably found among the larger birds of prey. For example the lammergeier (or bearded vulture) has a territory covering about 80 square miles (207 km^2), which it patrols to find the animal carcasses on which it feeds. The smallest territory is that of the common murre, pairs of which sometimes nest only a body width apart and in densities of up to four birds per square foot (0.09 m^2).

What determines the size of a bird's territory?

It used to be thought that the size of a territory increased relative to the size of the bird, but, although passerines do tend to have fairly small territories — anything from one-tenth of an acre to more than 10 acres (0.04–4.04 h) — so do colonial nesting species such as gannets. In fact the size of a territory is generally determined by the food supply: seabirds nesting on a rocky island can be close together because they have an abundant and accessible supply of fish on their doorstep. In a sense, a large colony like this occupies a collective territory.

How do birds defend a territory?

Strategies for protecting a territory vary from one bird to another. Seabirds use ritualized movements of the head and bill to warn off rivals; if they come too close for comfort, a swift peck usually gets the message across! Birds with large territories, such as raptors, patrol them regularly to make sure that a rival has not sneaked into their area. But by far the most common method of defending a territory is singing: more than half the world's birds are songbirds, and they use sound both to defend a territory and to attract a mate (see Chapter 7).

When do birds pair up?

Most species, especially songbirds, pair up on the male's breeding territory as a direct result of the male's song or display. Some birds, however, choose a mate well in advance, while still on their wintering grounds. This applies particularly to waterfowl: ducks, geese and swans display and form pair bonds well before the breeding season, often thousands of miles away from where they will eventually nest. The pair will then travel together to the breeding grounds, where they can begin the process of nesting immediately, without wasting valuable time on the preliminaries.

Do females play hard to get?

Yes, very much so. As with humans, courtship among birds is a complex series of games and strategies. At the start, the female often rejects the male's advances so that he becomes even more enthusiastic in his approach. Gradually she becomes more responsive, until she finally allows him to copulate with her and the pair is formed. She appears to be testing his fidelity and persistence: if he has to make such an effort to win her, perhaps he is less likely to be unfaithful!

Do females ever display to males?

Yes. In some species the female not only has a brighter plumage than the male, but also takes the lead in courtship, leaving the male to incubate the eggs and raise the young. Such species include all three phalaropes, the painted snipe and the dotterel.

Who finally chooses a mate — the male or female?

It used to be assumed that the male selects a mate — after all, he usually takes the lead in courtship display. Studies have revealed, however, that the female often makes the final choice of whether to accept or reject a suitor.

Do birds fight each other over a mate?

Some species get into serious squabbles. European robins are particularly aggressive, males sometimes even fighting to the death over territory or females.

How long do males and females stay together?

That depends. In fact almost every kind of relationship between the sexes occurs among birds. Thus a male and female may pair for life, as in the larger swans, or meet only a handful of times at a "lek" (see page 140), as in some species of grouse or manakin. Other birds stay together for several days, weeks or months; in some species males mate with several females, or the other way around. Despite these anomalies, however, the vast majority of birds form pairs for a breeding season or longer.

Size does matter!

The longest bird penis belongs to a specimen of the Argentine blue-billed duck (also known as lake duck), recently discovered by scientists from the University of Alaska. It measured 17 inches (43.18 cm) long, about the same length as the bird itself! The organ is corkscrew-shaped, allowing it to retract into the bird's body when not in use. It is thought that this extraordinary length is due to runaway sexual selection, where female preference drives male anatomy to ever greater extremes. Male blue-billed ducks are known to be promiscuous and have been described as "boisterous in their sexual activity." Incidentally, they belong to the group called "stifftails."

Do any birds pair for life?

A few do, the best-known example being the mute swan; in this species, usually only the death of one of the pair will end the partnership. In most species, however, the pair bond usually lasts for the length of the breeding season, and even then may be disrupted by infidelity or the taking of multiple partners. Pairing for life is usually found in birds that live for a very long time, such as albatrosses and large raptors.

Which species has the most bizarre courtship display?

There are many candidates for this honor. The short list would have to include the Guianan cock-of-the-rock from South America, in which the male displays his fabulous plumage to several females in a "court" inside a forest clearing; the larger albatrosses, which face each other and point their bills at the sky while making extraordinary noises; and the bowerbirds of Australasia, the males of which build ornate "bowers" decorated with all kinds of colorful objects to attract a female. These bizarre performances have one thing in common: they all work! Otherwise, of course, the performers would not be with us today.

Do some birds have more than one mate?

Yes, quite a number of bird species "play the field." A small minority are habitually "polygamous" — that is, a male mates with more than one female (polygyny), or a female mates with more than one male (polyandry). Polygyny is more common, occurring in about 2 percent of the world's bird species, primarily songbirds such as the marsh wren and red-winged blackbird. Polyandry is much rarer, occurring mainly in groups such as the phalaropes, in which the female is also brighter and more dominant than the male. A very few species indulge in "polygynandry," where several males mate with several females — the avian equivalent of "swinging." Various ratites, such as the ostrich, the emu and rheas, practice this.

The bowerbirds of Australia and New Guinea are skilled builders. To attract a mate, the male constructs a bower of plant material and décorates the entrance with a variety of colorful and sometimes shiny objects.

Can birds be unfaithful to their partner?

Yes, definitely. Although relatively few species are genuinely polygamous, many indulge in what might be described as "a bit on the side." A male does this to increase his total number of young, with the added advantage that chicks being raised in another male's nest do not require any work on the part of the biological father. The more chicks he manages to have, the more he furthers the continuation of his genetic line — which is really his principal purpose in life. A female may "play away" to optimize the quality of her offspring (by not laying all her eggs in one genetic basket, as it were). The result is that many males are unwittingly raising at least some young that are not their own. Recent studies have revealed that almost half the chicks in an indigo bunting's nest may not be the offspring of the resident male.

Building big

The largest nest made by any bird is that of one of the megapodes, the orange-footed scrubfowl of Australia. One breeding mound was estimated to measure roughly 60 feet (18 m) long, 16 feet (4.9 m) wide and 10 feet (3 m) high, and may have weighed as much as 50 tons (45 t)! The largest tree nest is that of the bald eagle. Enlarged annually, one nest in Florida measured 20 feet (6 m) deep by 10 feet (3 m) across, and weighed almost three tons (2.7 T) — the equivalent of three army jeeps! Of communal nesters, the African social weaver builds a colonial nest measuring up to 26 by 6 feet (7.9 by 1.8 m), with over 100 individual chambers.

So why do any birds bother with monogamy?

Monogamy works! It provides the female with a partner to share the hard labor of raising offspring, by taking his turn to incubate the eggs, feeding her while she is incubating and bringing food to the nest after the young have hatched. It also gives the male his best shot at raising a successful brood of young, and means he does not have to waste time and energy seeking out several prospective mates. In fact it has been estimated that about 90 percent of the world's birds are essentially monogamous (though at least some of these still grab other mating opportunities if they arise).

What is a "lek"?

A lek is a communal area in which males gather to perform public displays to attract watching females, who then choose the most impressive male. The term comes from a Swedish word meaning "to play." Lekking behavior is a bizarre adaptation because once a male has successfully mated with a female their paths will not cross again — thus she is left her to do all the work in raising a family. Such behavior has evolved in several parts of the world and among a wide range of families, including grouse, manakins, waders, some species of hummingbird and several different birds-of-paradise. It appears to occur only where the food supply is plentiful, which means males do not have to defend territories to find enough food for their offspring.

Is lekking unique to birds?

No. It is also practiced by several species of mammal, including antelopes, walruses and fruit bats.

How do birds actually mate?

As in humans, birds mate by engaging in a sexual act known as copulation. Normally the male mounts the female, and they maneuver around until the male's cloaca (a single opening beneath the tail used both for excretion and reproduction) engages with that of the female. Sperm is then passed from the male into the female, where it fertilizes her eggs. Incidentally, birds' sexual organs shrink dramatically outside the breeding season to reduce their weight for optimal flying.

Where do they do it?

Most birds mate either on the ground or while perching, as this maximizes the chances of success. Many waterbirds, however, such as ducks, will copulate in the water, while a few, such as swifts, even manage to do it in flight!

Are any birds gay?

Not in the strict human sense of engaging solely in sexual relationships with a partner of the same sex. As with mammals, though, male birds will sometimes mount another male as if to copulate. This may be a case of mistaken identity (especially in species where males and females resemble each other), an act of aggression or simply an outburst of sexual frustration. It occurs most often among colonial nesters, especially gulls, where there is an imbalance between the sexes.

Do birds ever mate with others from a different species?

Yes, frequently, although such pairings do not always produce off-spring. "Hybridization," as it is known, generally occurs between individuals of two closely related species whose genetic makeup is similar. The practice is particularly common among certain groups, especially ducks and geese, among which more than 400 different hybrid combinations have been observed — causing much confusion among birders!

Do hybrid offspring look more like one parent than the other?

Sometimes, yes. For example, any hybrids involving a Canada goose tend to show the distinctive dark head and pale face patch of that species. Otherwise they often show an equal mixture of characteristics, enabling an observer to work out their origin. In a few rare cases a hybrid will show a plumage feature that does not appear to come from either parent, the result of an ancestral characteristic revealing itself.

What becomes of the hybrid young?

The offspring of such pairings are usually infertile, and therefore do not last more than a single generation. However, some hybrids not only are fertile, but demonstrate a process known as "hybrid vigor" — that is, are more fertile than their parents. This often occurs in captivity, where poultry or cage birds are deliberately crossbred to create newer, "better," strains. It can also happen in the wild, as when various species of Darwin's finches on the Galápagos hybridized during unusual weather conditions brought about by the weather system known as "El Niño." These hybrids had larger bills, which proved better suited to the new conditions, and as a result thrived in competition with their parent species. Scientists are still puzzling over the implications of this extraordinary event for our definition of what makes a species.

NESTS

What is a nest?

In its broadest sense, a nest is simply a place where an egg or eggs are laid, the young hatch and, in some species, where the chicks are brooded until they are ready to leave.

Bijou residence

The smallest nests are those of the tiniest members of the hummingbird family. The bee hummingbird's nest has been measured at less than 0.8 inch (2.03 cm) in diameter and depth.

Is nest building unique to birds?

No. Although birds are by far the best-known nest builders, other groups of animals also build nests. These include the king cobra, which drags dead vegetation into a small heap by using the coils of its body; several apes, notably the orangutan, which constructs large nests for sleeping and shelter from the rain; and a whole range of fish, spiders, turtles and even crocodiles. Perhaps the best-known nest builders other than birds were the dinosaurs.

Why build a nest?

All creatures that build nests do so for the same reasons: to protect the eggs and offspring from the elements, to safeguard them against predators and to create a convenient single location in which to tackle the tricky work of incubating eggs and feeding young.

How many different kinds of nest are there?

About a dozen different basic nest designs exist, and each species fashions its own particular variation. The simplest nest is just a scrape in the ground, such as gulls and waders make, or even a natural depression in a rock, which many colonial seabirds use. This is hardly a nest at all in the traditional sense, since it involves no construction, yet to the bird it is just as important as the ornate edifices other species build. A more typical nest is the cup- or bowl-shaped nest favored by the majority of songbirds. This is usually made from grass or twigs and lined with vegetation or mud — or a variety of other materials including lichen, spiderswebs and even saliva! Many species, from the world's smallest hummingbirds to the bald eagle, use this highly versatile design. The next most popular design, which everything from woodpeckers to owls and tits to trogons use, is a hole, either a cavity in a tree or a burrow made in earth or sand.

What about more unusual nests?

Other, less conventional designs include floating nests (e.g., grebes, coots) nests stuck to the sides of buildings (e.g., house martin) and the giant mounds built by the megapodes — gamebirds that pile up decomposing vegetable matter in which to incubate their eggs. More complex structures include domed nests, such as those that various tropical songbirds create to protect their eggs and chicks from the sun, some of which, including that of the Cape penduline-tit, even incorporate a false entrance to confuse predators. The most complex nest of all is arguably the enormous multichambered structure that the sociable weaver, of the Kalahari region of southern Africa, creates, which may contain as many as 100 individual nests.

The killdeer, a kind of plover, leaves its well-camouflaged eggs out in the open. They are very difficult to locate even when you know the nest is in the area.

Various species of African weavers nest colonially. In some species, the birds build many nests in the same tree, often on the same branch; in other species, the colony creates one large "apartment" structure containing a chamber for each pair.

The nest mounds of scrubfowl, members of the Megapode family, have been reported to be as large as 35 feet wide and 15 feet high.

Do all birds have a nest?

No. The fairy tern precariously balances its egg on a horizontal branch and the male emperor penguin incubates its single egg on the upper side of its feet, keeping it warm by covering it with a special fold of skin. The alternative would be to lay its egg on the surface of the ice, where it would rapidly freeze!

Do both sexes build the nest?

Nest building varies from one species to another. In the majority of species the female does most of the nest building, though in many species the male and female share the work equally. In some species one sex does the lot: for example, the male winter wren may build up to eight different "cock's nests," which the fussy female then inspects carefully until she is satisfied with a particular one.

How long does nest building take?

That depends on the complexity of the structure. Some nests, such as those that colonial seabirds use, barely require "building" at all, whereas the most complicated structures, such as those of the megapodes, may take several weeks to build. Most songbirds typically take between three and nine days to construct a nest, not much time when you consider, for example, that the European long-tailed tit's nest may contain up to 2,300 feathers!

Are some nests better built than others?

In the case of the typical cup-shaped nest, the soundness of its structure is critical to the breeding success of the occupants. A badly built nest will probably not survive bad weather or an inquisitive predator, while a well-made one can stand up to almost anything. Experience is vital: older birds tend to be better builders, as they have learned the complex skills of weaving nest material into a strong structure. For them, practice really does make perfect.

How do birds remember where their nest is?

As with finding their way on migration, birds use a number of both innate and learned cues to relocate their nest site. This process can be extraordinarily rigid. When scientists moved a gull's eggs a few feet outside the nesting scrape, the adult bird returned to the original nest site and proceeded to brood in the very same place, ignoring the eggs nearby. This proves that it is fidelity to the site, rather than to the actual eggs, that matters.

Do birds build more than one nest?

As well as the habit of some birds — such as the winter wren — of building several nests to offer females a choice, birds commonly abandon a half-completed or even finished nest and start again elsewhere. This usually happens when the adults get wise to something that might harm their breeding success, such as the presence of a predator or disturbance by humans. Some species of weaver are known to build "decoy nests" to fool predators such as snakes.

Do birds build a new nest every year?

Most do. Indeed even species that have two or three broods in a single season usually build a new nest for each one, though they may take material from the old nest. Others, including many large eagles, continue to add to the old nest year after year until it becomes a truly enormous structure.

Why do some birds breed in colonies and others alone?

Nesting in a colony, together with several hundred (sometimes many thousands of) other birds, has several obvious advantages. The main one, as with flocking and communal roosting (see Chapter 5) is safety in numbers: by being part of a mass of birds, each individual dramatically reduces its chances of falling victim to a predator. This is particularly important for seabirds, whose young stay in the nest for several weeks or months and would be very easy to attack if the bird nested alone. The food supply around a colony is usually abundant so that no advantage is to be gained in nesting apart from other birds.

So why don't all birds nest in colonies?

As always, what suits one particular bird will not necessarily suit another. Colonial nesting has its downsides, including more competition for mates, a greater struggle for food and space, and a higher risk of disease. Ironically, colonies are also more visible to predators, though the risk to individuals may still not be as high as it would be if they nested alone. Colonial nesters such as gannets also use up a lot of energy in skirmishes and occasional all-out fights with their neighbors.

How common is colonial nesting?

Not very: only about one in eight of the world's bird species nest in colonies. Among some groups, however, it is very common: more than 9 out of 10 species of seabird nest colonially.

Do some birds deliberately nest alongside other kinds of bird?

Yes. Apart from the obvious case of colonial species, some birds deliberately seek out another species when they choose a nest site. Long-tailed ducks for example, often nest in Arctic tern colonies, where they gain from these noisy and aggressive birds the advantage of protection against predators. Most bizarre of all, geese may stay safe from other predators by nesting alongside raptors such as peregrines or snowy owls.

Do birds ever use the nest of another species?

Yes, frequently. Large structures such as white storks' nests often host smaller "squatters" such as sparrows, while some species habitually take over the nests of other birds. Crows, for example, often usurp a bird of prey's nest, sometimes evicting the rightful owners in the process. But the most inviting nest to squatters appears to belong to a peculiar storklike bird called the hamerkop, found throughout sub-Saharan Africa. The hamerkop builds a huge structure out of mud, sticks and other debris in a tree fork, and intruders — including Egyptian geese, eagle owls and even monitor lizards — often arrive before the building is complete.

Do birds nest near other wild creatures?

Some birds will seek a measure of protection by nesting alongside other wild creatures. Certain tropical songbirds, such as blue wax-bills, nest beside colonies of aggressive biting or stinging insects, presumably because their proximity affords the birds protection against any predator trying to attack the nest. In Africa, the water dikkop (a close relative of the stone-curlew) often nests near croco-diles, again as a means of protection. Finally, many species live close to (or even in the homes of) human beings, either to take advantage of ready-made nest sites or possibly to gain protection. Examples include the aptly named house sparrow, barn swallow and barn owl, as well as various members of the crow and pigeon families.

EGGS AND INCUBATION

Do all birds lay eggs?

Yes. Birds are the only class of vertebrate that never gives birth to live young, although the majority of amphibians, fish and reptiles also lay eggs. Three primitive mammals, the duck-billed platypus, and two species of echidna (known collectively as monotremes), lay eggs too.

Why do birds lay eggs?

The egg is one of nature's best ways of providing protection and food to a growing chick. But the question remains, why don't birds do as

Eggstraordinary!

The largest egg laid by any living bird is that of the ostrich, whose egg measures an average of 6 inches (15.24 cm) long and 5 inches (12.7 cm) in diameter, and weighs about 3.3 pounds (1.5 kg) — roughly 24 times the size of an average hen's egg. It takes about 45 minutes to hard-boil an ostrich egg!

The largest egg ever laid was that of the extinct elephant bird of Madagascar, whose egg weighed up to 26.5 pounds (12.02 kg) and measured 15 by 12 inches (38.1 by 30.48 cm) — about eight times the size of an ostrich egg. Some scientists believe the elephant bird's egg to have been larger than any dinosaur egg.

The largest egg of any North American bird is laid by the trumpeter swan and measures an average of 4.75 inches (12.07 cm) long, weighing about 14 ounces (396.9 g).

the vast majority of mammals and keep the young safe in the mother's body until the young are born? The reason is related to the fact that birds generally are lighter for their size than other creatures, due to their need to fly. So the extra weight of the young birds inside a mother's body would make it difficult — perhaps impossible — for her to get airborne and would increase her risk of being eaten by predators. Because the female bird lays eggs, usually in a nest, the male, at least in some species, can share in the process of rearing a family.

How many eggs do birds lay?

This varies enormously from one family of birds to another. A few (many seabirds) lay just a single egg; others (hummingbirds, most birds of prey) lay 2; many (most songbirds, waders etc.) lay between 3 and 6; some (certain smaller songbirds, including tits) lay 7 to 12; and a small minority (gamebirds such as pheasants, partridges and quails) lay a dozen or more. If eggs are continually removed from a nest, however, some birds will continue laying almost indefinitely. Hence the popularity of domesticated ducks and chickens!

Why do some birds lay more eggs than others?

This depends mainly on two factors: the likely survival rate of the young, and how much effort it takes to raise them. Large, long-lived colonial nesters such as the wandering albatross lay only a single egg and devote all their efforts to raising the chick over a very long period (about nine months from hatching to fledging). Songbirds, which have a very high death rate and a short lifespan, tend to lay large clutches to maximize the chances of one or two chicks reaching adulthood. It is interesting to note that resident species such as tits and nuthatches tend to have larger clutches than migratory species such as warblers, suggesting that migration is less hazardous than staying put for the winter.

How soon after fertilization is an egg laid?

The actual process following fertilization, which includes the deposition of the albumen, the formation of the membranes and the formation and coloration of the eggshell, takes roughly 24 hours for most species.

Eggstraordinary! *cont.*

The largest egg relative to body size is laid by the little spotted kiwi of New Zealand, whose egg weighs just under 10 ounces (383.5 g), almost one-quarter of the body weight of the female, and the equivalent, in proportion to the layer's weight, of an ostrich egg weighing 55 pounds (24.95 kg)!

The smallest egg is probably that laid by the world's smallest bird, the bee hummingbird, which measures about 0.5 inch long by 0.33 inch in diameter (1.3 by 0.84 cm) and weighs 0.02 ounce (0.57 g) — equivalent to about half a paper clip! It would take 125 bee hummingbird eggs to equal the weight of a hen's egg, and an incredible 3,000 to equal the weight of an ostrich's.

The smallest egg relative to body weight is that laid by the emperor penguin, which at just over 1 pound (0.45 kg) is just 1.5 percent of the adult's body weight of 66 to 88 pounds (29.94–39.92 kg), and the ostrich, whose egg also weighs roughly 1.5 percent of the adult's body weight.

Sitting tight

The longest incubation period belongs to the wandering and royal albatrosses (from 75 to 85 days, but not continuously) and the brown kiwi (up to 85 days), while the longest continuous stretch of incubation is that of the male emperor penguin, which keeps a single egg warm by resting it on his feet for up to 67 days without a break. Among passerines, the lyrebirds incubate their single egg the longest, for about 50 days. The shortest incubation period is probably that of the red-billed quelea (the world's most numerous bird), which can be as short as 10 days.

Is a clutch of eggs laid all at once?

The most common pattern of egg-laying is one egg every 24 hours, found among songbirds, most ducks and geese, and smaller waders. Birds of prey, ostriches and larger shorebirds usually lay their eggs two or three days apart, while for some seabirds the gap is even longer — up to a week in the case of the masked booby.

Do birds lay eggs at a particular time of day?

Many birds, including songbirds and hummingbirds, lay their eggs at dawn. This means they can immediately feed and gain the energy necessary to lay the next one. Pigeons and pheasants, however, tend to lay in the evening.

Are all eggs the same shape?

No. In fact some are not even egg-shaped! The eggs of owls and kingfishers are almost round, while those of grebes and loons are long and thin. Common murre's eggs are "pear-shaped" (rounded at one end and tapered at the other), which reduces their chances of falling off narrow cliff ledges since eggs of this shape tend to spin in a tight circle when knocked. Many waders also lay pear-shaped eggs, as these fit snugly together when laid in a clutch of four, making them easier to incubate.

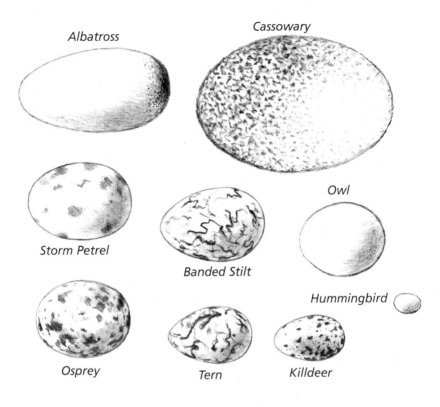

The size, color and patterning of birds' eggs vary a great deal, and not all are "egg-shaped," that is, having one end more pointed than the other.

Do large birds lay big eggs and small birds lay small ones?

In actual terms, yes, but not in relative terms. In fact, as a general rule, egg weight as a proportion of the female's body weight declines the larger a bird is, so that whereas the eggs of most songbirds weigh about 10 to 20 percent of the female's body weight, those of the ostrich weigh less than 2 percent of hers.

Why are some eggs white, while others are patterned or colored?

In general, eggs are colored or patterned to help disguise them from predators, and white when laid in holes, where predators are unlikely to be hunting by sight. White eggs may also be easier for the adult bird to see in the dark. It is thought that birds' eggs were originally white (like those of their reptile ancestors) and later developed colors and patterns as the need for concealment increased. Common patterns include spotting, marbling, streaking and blotching.

How long does incubation take?

This varies a lot, from just 10 days in the case of the red-billed quelea of Africa to almost three months in the case of the larger albatrosses and the brown kiwi of New Zealand. Most songbirds incubate for between two and three weeks, ducks and waders do so for slightly longer (three to four weeks) and raptors, geese and swans incubate for still longer periods (four to six weeks).

Do male birds incubate?

Yes, in many species both males and females incubate the eggs. In a small minority of species, however, the males do it alone, with no direct help from the female. These include various species of jacana and phalarope, and the emperor penguin of Antarctica.

Why do birds abandon their eggs?

Any bird may abandon its nest and eggs for a number of reasons, including predation, bad weather or disturbance. Better safe than sorry — after all, there's always next year. The megapodes of Southeast Asia and Australasia, though, have made desertion a way of life. They build enormous mounds of vegetation in which they bury their eggs, relying on the heat that the rotting vegetation generates to incubate them. Young megapodes hatch fully feathered and can look after themselves immediately, never knowingly meeting their parents. The same, of course, is true of young brood parasites such as cuckoos (see below).

What is an "addled" egg?

One that has failed to hatch because the embryo has died.

What is an "infertile" egg?

An egg that was never fertilized so does not contain an embryo. Unmated females sometimes lay infertile eggs.

Do eggs in a clutch all hatch at the same time?

That depends. In many species, especially songbirds, incubation does not begin until there is a full clutch, so most eggs will hatch on the same day. Other birds, such as raptors, take a different approach: of two golden eagle eggs, generally one will hatch a couple of days before the other, with the result that the elder chick tends to be larger and healthier than the other. This is an insurance policy for the adults: in a poor year for hunting, they will mainly feed the larger chick and the younger one will die; in a year when food is abundant, both chicks will survive. Although this strategy seems cruel, it is a sensible one: better that one strong chick survives than that both die of starvation.

Do birds ever lay their eggs in other birds' nests?

Yes, frequently. When population density is high (as in colonial species), this practice is especially common. The interloper can thus increase the number of offspring to which it passes on its genes, without having to go through the tedious business of actually raising them.

What is a "brood parasite"?

Technically, any species that lays an egg in another bird's nest. The term is usually reserved, however, for those habitual cheats, such as

An easy lay

The most eggs produced during a single breeding season is 40, by the female brown-headed cowbird of North America. The reason for this impressive productivity is that the cowbird is a brood parasite, laying her eggs in other birds' nests, so she does not have to incubate eggs or raise the young.

several species of cuckoo and cowbird, which always lay their eggs in the nests of a different species, letting the host parents do all the work of raising the young. This enables the female brood parasite to lay far more eggs than would normally be possible (up to 40 in a single breeding season) and maximizes the bird's chances of producing plenty of offspring.

How do the eggs fool the host species?

The innate urge to incubate eggs is a very strong one, which means that the host birds are already inclined to do so. The intruder may improve the odds for its own eggs, however, by making them as close as possible in shape, color and size to the eggs of its host. The cuckoo, for example, lays very different color eggs depending on which species it chooses as its host. This can lead to an evolutionary "arms race" in which, as the hosts get better and better at detecting the intruder's egg, only those eggs closest in appearance to their own survive, becoming even harder to detect than before.

Why don't hosts reject chicks that are not their own?

Once the chick is hatched, the stimulus of an open mouth requiring food appears to be enough to fool almost any parent. This persists even when the young bird has grown to more than twice the size of the adult host (as in the case of the common cuckoo and the dunnock).

A cowbird nestling, which competes with its foster siblings for food, may quickly outgrow them. Cowbird brood parasitism jeopardizes the breeding success of many songbird species.

How many brood parasites are there?

About 1 percent of the world's birds are brood parasites (roughly 100 species). The phenomenon occurs in six families: the majority of Old World cuckoos and three species of New World cuckoos, five of the six species of cowbird, most of the honeyguides of Africa and Asia, some African whydahs and widowbirds, indigobirds and a single species of wildfowl — the black-headed duck of South America. This wide range of families shows that the habit must have evolved independently in several places.

HATCHING, BROODING AND FLEDGING

How does a chick hatch?

As the embryo grows, it develops a sharp projection known as an egg tooth on its bill and a hatching muscle at the back of its skull; at the same time the eggshell becomes weaker, and an air space develops at the blunt end of the egg. Once the chick is ready to emerge, it pushes itself up to the blunt end, cracking the shell with its egg tooth. Then it uses its legs to move itself around the egg, producing tiny cracks in the shell. Finally it pushes itself out and emerges into the world, exhausted but free! This process usually takes a few hours, but may take anything from 30 minutes (most songbirds) to several days (albatrosses). The egg tooth falls off after a few days.

What is "brooding"?

The sitting on chicks by one or both parent birds to keep them warm and safe against predators. The term is also sometimes used as a synonym for incubation, that is, sitting on eggs.

What is "fledging"?

This is the process by which a baby bird becomes ready to leave the nest and fly. It takes place in several stages: while the young-ster is in the nest it is a "nestling"; when it leaves the nest but cannot yet fly and is still being fed by its parents, it is a "fledgling"; and it is only "fully fledged" when it has shed its down, acquired a full set of feathers and flown the nest. The term "fledging" applies mainly to birds such as songbirds, whose the young are born help-less and stay in the nest for a period before they acquire their first full plumage.

Why do some birds leave the nest more quickly than others?

The young of many kinds of bird are much more independent after hatching than those of other species. They are able to leave the nest almost straight away and can walk or swim and, in many cases, find food for themselves. These are known as "precocial" species and include all wildfowl, waders and gamebirds. Most of these birds nest on the ground, where being able to look after oneself is an urgent survival priority. Other groups, such as gulls, are "semi-precocial," having young that are active but remain in the nest and are fed by their parents; herons and owls are less self-reliant and are known as "semi-altricial" species. All songbirds, in contrast, are "altricial": they are born naked and blind and their parents must feed them until they are fully fledged (see above). Another term for precocial is "nidifugous," while the corresponding term for altricial is "nidicolous."

What should I do if I find a baby bird that has fallen out of its nest?

Leave it alone! The parents are almost certainly close by and able to take care of it themselves. If you take it into your home, the bird is highly likely to die. The only exception to this rule is if you find a naked, helpless nestling that has just fallen out of its nest; in that case, put it straight back in the nest and hope for the best. Try to handle the nestling as little as possible.

Which birds feed their young for the longest period after fledging?

Some seabirds, including frigatebirds, may feed their young for as long as 18 months after they fledge. This species steals food from other seabirds and then regurgitates it for their offspring.

Leaving home

The longest fledging period is that of the king penguin, at up to 13 months. Of flying birds, the wandering albatross takes up to 280 days (just over 9 months). The shortest fledging period is 9 days, found in several passerines, including the corn bunting.

Which bird is the most sociable nester?

The aptly named sociable weaver of Africa, which builds an enormous collective nest with up to 100 separate chambers; such a nest insulates the eggs and young against freezing winter nights in the Kalahari desert. The largest nests are over a metre high and several metres in diameter, and may house over 300 birds at any one time.

How do birds keep their nest clean?

Many birds remove their offspring's droppings, which come enclosed in "fecal sacs" (shrink-wrapped poop, if you like!) to avoid soiling the nest. Others are less house proud, allowing the feces to build up, which in tropical climates can cause quite a stink. Arguably the dirtiest nesters of all are the hornbills, in which the female uses a mixture of mud and her own droppings to wall herself into the nest cavity (sometimes with help from her partner), where she stays throughout the incubation and brooding period. She finally emerges in a very filthy state indeed.

How do young birds learn to fly?

Flight is an instinctive rather than a learned skill. A baby bird leaving a nestbox will, after some hesitation, launch itself out of the nest hole and into the air. While first flights are not always very successful or stylish, the birds soon get the hang of it. Other birds, such as young peregrines, will practice flapping their wings for several days before leaving the nest, thereby building up their wing muscles. Once airborne, they will also get "tuition" from their parents — the first step on the way to becoming supreme masters of the air.

9 WHERE DO BIRDS GO?

MIGRATION

What is "migration"?

Migration, at its simplest level, is defined as a regular seasonal movement of a population of organisms. Birds are probably the best known of these, but it is also a way of life for an amazing variety of other animals — from anchovies to zebras. Usually, though not always, migration takes place between breeding and wintering areas and involves two journeys each year, one outward and one return.

Why do birds migrate?

Birds migrate to find food and somewhere to breed, neither of which are available in one place all year round. Take a typical insect-eating migrant such as the blackpoll warbler. After breeding in the forests of Canada during the summer, it heads off on a journey of almost 6,200 miles (10,000 km) to South America to avoid the cold, foodless northern winter. There, it spends the winter (the South American summer) in a warm, sunny environment with plenty of insect food, before returning north in spring when conditions are once again suitable for breeding.

Isn't migrating riskier than staying put?

Although undertaking such a long journey may seem a risky strategy, the dangers of staying put for the winter, in a cold climate with little or no insect food, outweigh the dangers encountered on migration. Migration gives birds the best of both worlds. In fact perhaps a more apt question to ask is, why don't all birds migrate?

Why do some insectivorous birds stay put in the northern United States and Canada during the winter?

A few mainly insect-eating species, such as the black-capped and boreal chickadees, do remain in the northern forests all year round, despite the very low temperatures. They survive by exploiting hidden food sources, such as tiny insects hiding beneath the bark of trees. It is lack of food — not cold weather itself — that kills birds in winter.

So why do migrants bother coming back again?

Most songbird migrants from North America and Europe spend the winter in South or Central America and sub-Saharan Africa, respectively. But the abundant food supplies they find there do not last all year round. If these birds were to remain through to the breeding season, when extra energy is required to produce eggs and feed young, finding enough food might become difficult — especially given the degree of competition from local resident species. Birds that return to temperate areas such as North America tend to have larger clutches (and sometimes more broods) than birds in tropical regions. This all suggests that the plentiful food supply available in the northern summer allows these birds to enjoy a more successful breeding season than if they had remained in the tropics. The longer daylight hours of the northern summer also assist with the rearing and rapid growth of young birds, as there is more time to search for food.

Do all birds from one species migrate?

No. Some species are partial migrants, with different individuals following different strategies. For example, adult blue jays tend to stay in or near their breeding areas for the winter, while young birds may wander far and wide.

How did migration come about in the first place?

It is often said that migrating birds head south for the winter, but this puts the cart before the horse. In fact it is thought that many migratory birds evolved in equatorial regions, where competition with other species there caused birds to head north to avoid it. By migrating they could also take advantage of the long daylight hours and plentiful food supply of the northern summer. But they still had to return south again every winter when the bad weather closed in. Thus migration was the key that opened up new lands for birds. It soon became a viable way of life for many species.

Why do birds go so far?

Surely migrants heading north in spring would be better off stopping to breed in the southern states of the United States, rather than pressing on to the Arctic. Well, many of them do. But those that do travel to the arctic circle gain the advantage of even longer hours of daylight and less competition from other species. This explains why birds such as the red knot undertake a huge journey from the southern hemisphere to the edge of the Arctic to breed — food is abundant there, and far fewer species are competing for it.

What proportion of the world's birds is migratory?

Approximately 4,000 species — roughly 40 percent of the global total — are usually considered to be migratory, though not all undertake long-distance journeys. Of the 650 or so regular North American

Migrant midget

The smallest intercontinental migrant is the ruby-throated hummingbird of North America. Twice a year this tiny bird puts on astonishing fat reserves, doubling its weight from 0.125 to 0.25 ounces (3.54–7.09 g) so that it can migrate almost 600 miles (965 km) across the Gulf of Mexico, to and from its winter quarters in Central America.

breeding species, about 75 percent (almost 500 species) can be said to migrate, although well below half of these are truly long-distance migrants (to the tropics and South America).

How many individual birds migrate?

Of North America's 20 billion or so birds, it is thought that about one-third, or more than six billion individuals, migrate at least as far as Central America.

How do birds prepare for migration?

Birds prepare for migration in two ways. Most molt their worn adult feathers or first juvenal plumage, acquiring a spanking new set of feathers in preparation for the journey. They also build up fat reserves, which may take several weeks, as they feed frantically to increase their weight by up to 50 percent. The fat is stored in a layer just beneath the skin and is evident when migrating songbirds are caught for banding. A small songbird may increase its normal weight from 0.4 ounces (10 g) to as much as 0.6 ounces (15 g) during this period. Other birds, especially waders, will put on some fat before-hand but also stop to feed on the journey south, replenishing their energy resources as they go. Large birds of prey such as the osprey, however, are unable to fatten up for migration, as this would make them too heavy to fly long distances, so they stop off to feed at regular intervals en route.

Do birds know when to migrate?

The notion that birds somehow "know" when to migrate goes back at least as far as the Old Testament, where it is written that "the turtle-dove and the swallow and the crane observe the time of their coming." Especially in spring, it does seem that some species arrive on preset dates — as can be seen from the widespread folk-lore about the arrival times of familiar species such as the barn swallow. But birds don't follow a calendar — at least not in the sense that we understand it. Instead they respond automatically to certain natural stimuli.

What makes birds set off on migration?

The main impulse for departure both from wintering areas and breeding grounds is tiny changes in day length, which affect the bird's brain. The brain triggers the bird's endocrine system to produce hormones that stimulate it to prepare for the long journey ahead — for example, by increased feeding to build up fat reserves. Even cage birds may show signs of restlessness during spring and autumn, when their wild counterparts are migrating.

Does the weather affect departure times?

Yes, especially in autumn, weather conditions can play a big part in the timing of birds' departure south. While birds may be physically ready to leave, they need to use the best weather conditions for migration so may stay put if the weather is bad. Thus songbirds leaving eastern Canada will usually wait for the passing of a cold front with clear skies and following winds that help them on their way.

Does climate change affect bird migration?

In recent years, global climate change — and its impact on weather patterns and temperatures — apparently causes some birds to arrive earlier than usual in spring and stay later in autumn. It is still too early to say whether climate change will permanently alter the timing of bird migrations. Climate change is also affecting birds by reducing their habitat; for example, widespread drought in the Sahel Zone of western Africa has led to the desertification of large areas, depriving migrants of the vital green areas that sustain them on their long-haul journeys.

The climatic phenomenon known as "El Niño" is also having a major effect on both breeding and migrating birds, by dramatically changing the world's weather patterns, especially in the tropics.

Do all migrants arrive and depart at the same time?

No. Different species arrive and depart at different times on both outward and return migrations. In the northern United States and Canada, the earliest spring songbird migrants are yellow-rumped warblers, which generally pass through in March, while some species of warbler do not get back to their nesting grounds until mid-May. In autumn, many shorebirds head south in July and August, along with yellow warblers, whereas various species of thrush are still passing south along the eastern seaboard well into October and November. Regional differences occur too: the farther north you go, the later the migrants arrive in spring, and the earlier they depart in autumn.

How do migrating birds find their way?

This is one of the greatest of all natural mysteries. Birds use no single method to find their way; instead, most employ a number of orientational tools. The most important are Earth's magnetic field and visual compasses such as the sun (for daytime migrants) and the moon and stars (for nighttime ones). Other useful tricks include the ability to perceive polarized light (especially when clouds obscure the sun), and "vector navigation" — similar to the "point-and-compass" method used by early sailors.

How do birds use Earth's magnetic field?

It has long been known that birds possess some form of internal compass, which enables them to detect Earth's magnetic field and use it to orientate themselves in the right direction. Scientists have discovered a substance called magnetite in the skulls of pigeons, which must enable them to sense their position in this way. Experiments have also shown that birds respond to an artificial magnetic field, which can be used to confuse their normal senses.

How do birds know when they have reached their destination?

As birds near their destination, visual landmarks such as coastlines, rivers and mountain ranges, wind direction, and sound and smell come into play, allowing birds to return, in some cases, to the very place where they were born. Of course, such landmarks don't help when young birds are making the journey for the first time — which just demonstrates the additional importance of a genetically inherited mental map.

What is a "passage migrant"?

A passage migrant is a species that passes through a particular area in spring and autumn but generally does not stay to breed or winter there. How you define a passage migrant, however, depends on where you are standing at the time: the ruddy turnstone is a passage migrant throughout much of its range but is a breeding visitor to the Arctic and a nonbreeding visitor to the coasts of Africa and South America.

Air miles

The world's longest migratory journey is undertaken by the Arctic tern, from its sub-Arctic breeding grounds to and from the Antarctic — an annual round-trip of up to 22,000 miles (35,400 km). During its lifetime, a single bird may travel more than 500,000 miles (805,000 km) — more than any other species. As a result, the Arctic tern experiences more daylight than any other living creature. One individual, banded as a chick near Murmansk in Russia, was recaptured alive a year later near Fremantle in Western Australia — more than 14,000 miles (22,500 km) away.

The longest journeys of land birds include those made by the barn swallow, which migrates in the New World from Alaska to Argentina, and in the Old World between Norway and South Africa — both journeys of roughly 6,000 miles (9,700 km) each way. But this is dwarfed by the journey of the white-throated needletail, a species of swift, which undertakes a twice-yearly trip between Siberia and Tasmania of roughly 7,500 miles (12,000 km) each way.

How long do birds' migratory journeys take?

Many smaller migrants, such as the red knot, work on the "long-hop" system, covering hundreds of miles a day and reaching their destination in just a few days. Others, including the osprey, take their time, stopping off to feed for a few hours or even days before restarting their journey south, and taking several months to reach their destination.

How high do migrating birds fly?

Different groups migrate at different altitudes: raptors at around 2,000 to 3,300 feet (600–1,000 m), most songbirds at below 5,000 feet (1,500 m), and waders and geese at 5,000 to 10,000 feet (1,500–3,000 m).

Incredible as it may seem, bar-headed geese migrate over the Himalayas at altitudes where winds and cold temperatures are extreme and little oxygen is available.

Occasionally birds venture even higher: there are records of migrating wildfowl and raptors topping 20,000 feet (6,000 m).

Do birds migrate by night as well as day?

Yes, very much so. In fact more species — and many more individuals — are night flyers, and for several reasons. First, the air is cooler at night, which is especially important as the bird goes farther south. Cool air allows a bird to fly faster, with less dehydration and loss of energy. Second, fewer predators are around at night, as most are daytime migrants. Finally, migrating by night and stopping by day allows birds to feed and rest during daylight hours. Nocturnal migrants include most songbirds, wildfowl and waders.

Why do some birds migrate by day?

Birds that can feed "on the go," such as swallows and swifts, generally migrate by day, feeding on flying insects on the way. Other diurnal migrants include birds of prey, which because of their weight and soaring style of flight rely on thermals (rising currents of warm air) to gain altitude for migration.

Why do some birds migrate in a V-formation?

Some larger birds, notably swans, geese and cranes, often travel in a V-formation. This is an energy-efficient way for them to cover large distances, as the leading bird creates uplift and reduces wind friction for the others (just like racing cyclists riding in a pack). The lead bird is usually an experienced adult and will take turns with others to avoid becoming exhausted.

Do all migratory birds follow the same route?

As you might expect, different species follow very different routes. Raptors such as eagles and buteos find flying over large expanses of water difficult because of the lack of thermal air currents to give them lift. So most migrant North American birds of prey take the land route south, passing through the Isthmus of Panama to reach South America.

Do young and adult birds all travel together?

Not always. Although some groups of birds, notably cranes and wild-fowl, often travel in family groups, the young of most other species are left to their own devices. Many adult waders and songbirds leave several weeks earlier than the juveniles, which must undertake their first journey without help. The most extreme example of this is the juvenile Eurasian cuckoo, whose parents abandon it even before birth! Yet despite the lack of parental guidance, these species are no less successful than those in which adults and young travel together. This shows that many orientational techniques are innate, rather than learned.

Do birds coming back in spring follow their autumn route in reverse?

Most do, but a few species undertake what is known as loop migration. In North America, many species of wood-warbler travel across the western Atlantic Ocean in autumn, taking advantage of tailwinds to follow the shortest possible route south. But in spring, when there are no winds to help them on their way, they must follow a longer route along the eastern seaboard of the United States.

Do any birds migrate north for the winter?

In Africa and South America, quite a few species that breed in the southern hemisphere head toward the equator outside the breeding season, but in North America and Europe only a handful of species actually head north. They include Heerman's gull, which breeds in Mexico but travels northward each autumn to spend the winter along the Pacific coast of the United States and Canada as far as British Columbia. But perhaps the most extraordinary example of all is the

Ross's gull, which breeds in Arctic Canada and Siberia yet still heads north outside the breeding season to spend the winter on the edge of the Arctic pack ice!

What is "altitudinal migration"?

As opposed to "latitudinal migration," in which birds head roughly south or southwest in autumn and north or northeast in spring, altitudinal migration occurs when birds breeding at high altitudes head down toward lowland areas for the winter. They do so in search of a milder climate and more ample food supplies, which often means wintering on or near a sea coast. Although these journeys may seem insignificant in terms of distance traveled, they often involve a major change of lifestyle. Altitudinal migrants in North America include the mountain chickadee and Clark's nutcracker.

Long haul

The longest single migratory flight is probably that of the bar-tailed godwit, from its breeding grounds in southwest Alaska to New Zealand. The birds may make this journey, a distance of almost 6,800 miles (10,900 km), in a single flight. Other waders such as the bristle-thighed curlew and Pacific golden plover also undertake vast long-hops across the Pacific Ocean.

Do all migrants make regular twice-annual journeys?

No, a few species are irruptive, meaning that they undertake occasional and unpredictable mass movements away from their breeding areas. These movements are normally a result of food shortages on the birds' breeding grounds, sometime combined with a population boom. Irruptive species may be rare or absent one year, and abundant the next. They include various species of crossbill, which generally migrate in midsummer and often stay put for a year or more, breeding in their new location before returning to their original one.

Can birds change their migratory habits?

Yes, from time to time. A well-known example is the German population of the blackcap, which within a few decades changed its winter quarters from Iberia and North Africa to Britain and Ireland. This occurred as a result of a genetic mutation that sent birds in a north-westerly direction in autumn instead of a southwesterly one. Once on their new wintering grounds they found a mild climate and abundant food, enabling them to survive and return earlier to breed. As a result the mutant gene spread rapidly through the population, the whole of which now winters in Britain and Ireland.

Do migrating birds ever get lost?

Frequently, and for all sorts of reasons. In autumn, the vast majority of migrants are juveniles on their very first journey south. Their lack of experience means they can easily become disoriented, especially when they hit bad weather. Wind and rain may prevent them from using visual cues such as the sun or stars, so they tend to drift off course.

What happens to lost birds?

Many end up exhausted and fall to the ground or into the sea and drown; others allow themselves to be carried by crosswinds until they reach the safety of land. These birds generally reorient themselves and get back on course. But every autumn a few North American land birds get blown off course by westerly gales, cross the Atlantic and make landfall in Britain and Ireland, much to the delight of avid birdwatchers in the United Kingdom!

What is a "vagrant"?

In effect a vagrant is any wild bird found outside its normal range — either breeding, migratory or wintering — having arrived by natural means. There are several reasons for vagrancy, including unreliable orientation mechanisms, genetic mutations and the effects of extreme weather conditions. Vagrancy is most common among juvenile birds undertaking their first journey and so happens more often in autumn than spring, though it can occur at any time of year.

What is an "accidental"?

A vagrant. This term used to apply strictly to a bird that had occurred fewer than 20 times outside its normal range, but the definition has since become more flexible and can now mean any bird found outside its normal range.

What goes up …

The shortest migratory journeys are probably those made by altitudinal migrants such as the mountain quail and Clark's nutcracker of North America, which simply descend from the mountaintops to sheltered valleys during the autumn, and return to the high tops in spring. Mountain quail make the twice-yearly journey on foot!

Can good weather cause vagrancy?

Ironically, good weather can also lead to vagrancy. In spring, especially when high pressure brings fine, settled weather to the eastern seaboard of the United States, southern species such as swallow-tailed and Mississippi kites may drift farther north than usual and be seen at migration hotspots such as Cape May in New Jersey.

Apart from the weather, why else would a migrant go off course?

Other reasons for vagrancy include a kind of wanderlust, as when young nonbreeding birds simply "go flyabout" and end up outside their normal range. This may have an evolutionary advantage and eventually result in the species extending its breeding range.

Do vagrants ever find their way back home?

Not very often. Overshooting birds may well return south almost immediately, or spend the spring and summer in their new home before heading back to their winter quarters in the autumn. But for birds that have crossed the Atlantic from North America to Europe, prevailing westerly winds make the return journey virtually impossible. Most songbirds perish soon after arriving, due to lack of suitable food, but some larger species, such as waders and gulls, survive for many years, possibly migrating back and forth between Europe and Africa, instead of between North and South America.

After storms, birders are on the alert for species such as the albatross, that have been blown off course and show up at locations where normally they do not appear.

What is "abmigration"?

This occurs when an individual from one population or species accidentally joins a flock of another population or species, and migrates with the flock to their wintering areas. The following spring the disoriented bird usually stays with its new companions and therefore returns to a different breeding area. Abmigration often occurs among sociable migrants such as geese; a snow goose, for example, may join a flock of Greenland white-fronted geese in western Greenland and end up in Scotland instead of Texas.

What is a "fallout"?

A fallout is the simultaneous arrival of large numbers of migrants (usually songbirds such as warblers, flycatchers and thrushes) as a result of rough weather that forces them to make landfall.

What is a "wreck"?

A wreck, as any sailor will tell you, usually involves a storm at sea. In the case of birds, it means a major displacement of seabirds, often as a result of autumn or winter gales. Onshore winds may blow normally pelagic species such as shearwaters, petrels or alcids far inland. Some will die as a result, but many can reorient themselves and find their way back to the open ocean.

10 HOW DO WE RELATE TO BIRDS?

BIRDS AND PEOPLE

BIRD NAMES

How did birds get their English names?

History doesn't record which imaginative individual first coined the word "blackbird." Like most common names, it simply arose from the everyday observations of ordinary people. Thus some birds are named for physical characteristics such as color (yellow warbler), size (great blue heron) or markings (yellowthroat); some for their voice (whip-poor-will); some for what they do (brown creeper); and others for where they live (barn swallow). Ornithologists later developed new techniques for naming less common species. These included borrowing foreign names, adapting scientific names (such as phalarope, which derives from the Latin *Phalaropus*, meaning "coot-footed"), commemorating the place where the bird was first found (Cape May warbler) or commemorating a colleague (Wilson's warbler).

How did birds get their scientific names?

This was a lot more systematic. The pioneer who developed the process of giving each bird (and indeed every other organism) a scientific name was Carl Linnaeus, an 18th-century Swedish botanist.

Linnaeus invented the system known as "binomial nomenclature" (see Chapter 2), which gave each species a unique combination of two names, the first indicating its genus and the second its species. For instance, while Brits and Americans may argue the merits of great northern diver and common loon, to scientists this bird will always be *Gavia immer*.

How many birds are named after people?

According to Bo Beolens and Michael Watkins, authors of *Whose Bird?* more than 2,500 different species or subspecies are named after people. The exact number is impossible to say, since the origins of some names remain shrouded in mystery. *Whose Bird?* covers 1,100 different individuals, many of whom — such as Alexander Wilson or Peter Simon Pallas — had several different species named after them. Not surprisingly the vast majority of these individuals are men. It took women centuries to get a foot in the door of science.

Are any birds named after women?

A few, but these women were mostly the wives, sisters, mistresses or daughters of famous men, rather than well-known ornithologists in their own right. Again this is simply a sign of the times — specifically the 18th and 19th centuries, when most birds were being named.

How many North American birds are named after people?

In their book *Audubon to Xantus*, Barbara and Richard Mearns discuss 80 North American species named after 65 people. William Swainson gave his name to three species (a hawk, thrush and war-bler), John Cassin to four (an auklet, a kingbird, a sparrow and a finch) and Alexander Wilson, the founding father of American ornithology, to five (a storm-petrel, plover, phalarope, warbler and snipe). Wilson is also commemorated in the scientific names of hooded and Canada warblers.

How do you get a bird named after you?

Simple: just go out and discover it and then persuade a fellow scientist to name it in your honor. You could do this by "collecting" a specimen of a new species in the field, or by spotting it among a pile of old museum skins. However you get your hands on it, just make sure that you write up the first formal scientific description. Unfortunately, very few new species remain undiscovered today, so immortalizing yourself in avian nomenclature is increasingly difficult. Why not try insects or plants? There are plenty of those out there just waiting to be discovered!

Who has the most species named after him?

Twenty-six people — all men, of course — have at least 10 different species or subspecies named after them. Of these, one was Dutch, one Italian, two French, three American, four German and a remarkable 15 British! The Brits, as you might expect, occupy the top three places in the list. The bronze medal goes to P.L. Sclater, first editor of the *Ibis* (Britain's oldest ornithological journal), with 19 species. Charles Darwin, with 21 birds, claims a respectable silver. But the undisputed gold medallist, with a grand total of 24 different birds, is Victorian bird artist John Gould. He even managed to name one — Mrs. Gould's sunbird — after his wife!

Were kites and cranes named after birds or vice versa?

As with flight itself, birds came first. So mechanical kites were named after their avian counterparts, whose twisting flight they resembled, while metal cranes got their name from the statuesque birds whose vertical posture they shared.

How many ornithologists gave their names to secret agents?

Only one, but a very famous one! Author Ian Fleming was a neighbor and close friend of the author of *Birds of the West Indies*, a certain Mr. James Bond. Legend has it that inspiration struck when Fleming glanced at his friend's book while searching for a name for 007. The rest is literary and cinematic history.

BIRDS AS FOOD AND PETS

What is a "domesticated" species?

A domesticated species is one that has been bred in captivity over time to produce some product useful to people, usually meat, eggs or feathers. This definition excludes birds kept purely for ornament, such as most cage birds, or for sport, such as hawks and falcons (though racing pigeons are usually considered to be domestic birds). In some cases, such as farmyard hens and geese, it is obvious that a bird is domesticated; in others, such as game birds or wildfowl bred and released for shooting, the boundary between domesticated and wild is not so clear. Typical domesticated species in North America include Chinese geese (from Asia), the mallard (from Europe, Asia and North America), the Muscovy duck (from South America) and various kinds of guinea fowl (from Africa). In some cases you can easily tell an individual's wild ancestry; in others, extensive crossbreeding or hybridization has made doing so all but impossible.

How many different bird species are domesticated?

Tricky question. Not only is domestication hard to define, but the variety of uses to which birds are put in different cultures also means that any list of domesticated species is likely to be incomplete. We can all agree on one though: the red junglefowl of Asia — today better known in deep-fried, casserole or McNugget form!

What is a "game bird"?

Strictly speaking, it is any species unfortunate enough to find itself a target, for sport, food or profit, though the term is most commonly used for members of the order Galliformes (such as pheasants, grouse and guinea fowl).

Apart from food, what else have we used birds for?

Throughout our history, human beings have exploited wild and domesticated birds in numerous ways. We have used feathers and skins for clothing (both ceremonial dress and fashion), oil from the body fat of seabirds for heating and cooking, and even beaks and feet as primitive jewellery. Perhaps the most enterprising exploiters of birds were the islanders of St. Kilda, off the northwestern coast of Scotland, who until the 1920s lived almost entirely by harvesting seabirds, which they used for food, fuel and clothing — even wearing entire gannet skins as slippers!

What about birds as pets?

Human beings have kept birds behind bars for many thousands of years — either for the beauty of their plumage or for their song. Our ancestors originally caught and kept common native song-birds. Then, as foreign travel and trade grew during the 18th and 19th centuries, tastes turned to more exotic species such as the canary (from the Canary Islands), the budgerigar (from Australia) and numerous small finches (mainly from Africa and Asia). Parrots, with their longevity and powers of speech, became a favorite companion for sailors — as for Long John Silver's famous sidekick in Robert Louis Stevenson's *Treasure Island*. Today a vast range of bird species, including many very rare ones, are kept in captivity.

Can all kinds of bird be kept in cages?

Almost any kind of bird can, theoretically at least, be kept in a cage. But keeping it alive is a different matter. For many specialized species, captivity would spell an early death. Some, such as swifts or albatrosses, spend most of their lives airborne, so a cage would be completely impractical — not to say fatal — for them. It is, of course, illegal to take species from the wild, and many rare birds cannot be legally imported or bought and sold.

Does the cage bird trade do birds any harm?

Sadly, yes, if the birds are taken directly from the wild. Although many cage birds are now bred in captivity, there is still a great demand for wild birds, especially species that are hard to breed. Unfortunately the most threatened species are often the prize targets of unscrupulous collectors, who will pay a fortune for illegally obtained specimens, such as rare Saker falcons in demand for hunting by falconers in several Middle Eastern countries. This fuels

Lots in a name

The longest English name of any bird is, at least in terms of complexity, the King-of-Saxony bird-of-paradise, which has six words and 26 letters. However, several other species have names with 30 or more letters, including Middendorff's grasshopper warbler, Abyssinian yellow-rumped seedeater and champion of them all, at 32 letters, northern long-tailed glossy-starling. Several now obsolete names were even longer and more complex, including Mrs. Forbes-Watson's black-flycatcher (now Nimba flycatcher), Ceylon orange-breasted blue-flycatcher (now Tickell's blue-flycatcher) and the Himalayan golden-backed three-toed woodpecker (now simply Himalayan flameback) — an incredible 40 letters long.

The illegal trade in birds poses a threat to many species, some of which are on the brink of extinction. Many captured birds die in transit. Efforts are being made internationally to curb such trade in birds and other animals.

a flourishing underground trade, in which everyone from local collectors to international cartels has a vested interest in avoiding detection.

Which species are most affected?

BirdLife International estimates that people exploit roughly 3 of every 10 globally threatened species in some way. Sometimes this is for food, but mostly it is for the cage bird trade. Families hit hardest include parrots and macaws, pigeons and doves, and pheasants. The world's black spots include Southeast Asia (especially China, Indonesia and the Philippines) and South America (especially Brazil).

How much is the cage bird trade worth?

Today the cage bird trade is too huge to quantify. But to put it in perspective, some observers have estimated that the global trade in wildlife products as a whole, including live specimens, is second only to that in illegal drugs. The latest estimate from CITES (the Convention on International Trade in Endangered Species) suggests that roughly 1.5 million live birds are bought and sold every year, at a value of approximately $60 million. Although this works out to only $40 per individual bird, the most sought-after species can cost far more: it is said that during the 1980s hyacinth macaws from Brazil were retailing at a cost of $8,000 each.

BIRDS IN CULTURE

Have we ever worshipped birds?

Of course! We've worshipped most things in our time, so why not birds? Many early cultures reserved a sacred place for birds, or at least birdlike deities. Among these were the god Quetzalcoatl, the "feathered serpent," which the Aztecs of central Mexico worshipped prior to the Spanish conquest, and various Egyptian gods, including Horus — often depicted with the body of a man and the head of a falcon. The Egyptians also worshipped the sacred ibis — hence its name!

Who painted the first bird?

Well, we don't know the actual artist, but cave paintings in southern Europe that date back at least 18,000 years depict recognizable images of owls and long-legged water birds (probably cranes, herons or storks).

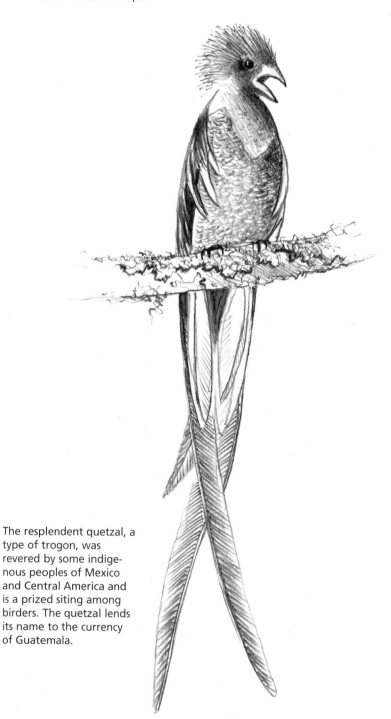

The resplendent quetzal, a type of trogon, was revered by some indigenous peoples of Mexico and Central America and is a prized siting among birders. The quetzal lends its name to the currency of Guatemala.

Which is the first bird mentioned in the Bible?

The raven, mentioned in the eighth chapter of the Book of Genesis: "And he sent forth a raven, which went forth to and fro, until the waters were dried up from off the earth." Noah seems to have kept no record of the actual species.

How many species are mentioned in the Bible?

Somewhere between 25 and 40 different kinds of bird make it into the Old and New Testaments, though problems with translation and lack of precision (e.g., "hawk," "owl") mean that we cannot be sure exactly how many species they represent. The dove is mentioned most — probably referring to the domesticated pigeon, although the turtle dove, a common migrant through the Holy Land, also crops up several times. Others include the stork, pelican and eagle, and even the ostrich — now extinct in the Middle East.

Tongue-twisters

The longest scientific name of any bird is that of the crowned slaty flycatcher from the Amazon basin in South America — *Griseotyrannus aurantioatrocristatus*. But this pales into insignificance beside the longest scientific name of any organism, that of a Russian amphipod (crustacean) — *Brachyuropskkyodermatogamm arus grievlinggwmnemnotus*.

There are several contenders for the shortest scientific name of any bird, each with only eight letters. These include Crex crex (corncrake), Tyto alba (barn owl) and Grus grus (common crane). But all these are beaten by the great evening bat of Southeast Asia, whose scientific name is just four letters long: *Ia io*.

How many species are mentioned in Shakespeare?

The Bard immortalized at least 50 kinds of bird , although the same caveats apply to them as to those mentioned in the Bible. Shakespeare often compared people to birds: in *Much Ado About*

Professional fowl

The earliest bird domesticated by humans was the red junglefowl of Asia, which was first domesticated in India more than 5,000 years ago. The ancient Egyptians also domesticated many animals, including the Egyptian goose, at least 4,000, and possibly as long as 4,500, years ago.

Nothing, he writes that "Beatrice, like a lapwing, runs, close by the ground," while Richard II has an eye "as bright as is the eagle's." Other bird references need a bit more deciphering, as in Hamlet's line "I know a hawk from a handsaw," in which the latter is a corruption of "hernshaw," meaning a young heron. For more detailed examples, see *Shakespeare's Birds* by Peter Goodfellow.

Which species are most popular in English poetry, and why?

The skylark and the nightingale both frequently crop up in the work of English poets — especially the Romantics, such as Shelley and Keats. They use these birds to evoke a particular mood, the skylark generally one of joy and optimism, and the nightingale one of mystery and melancholy.

Why are birds so popular in sayings and proverbs?

Probably because birds are among the most ubiquitous and visible aspects of the natural world, so people saw them more often than most other creatures and observed their appearance and habits more closely. Thus sayings such as "up with the lark" and "bald as a coot" have become part of our day-to-day language, and few people stop to consider their origins.

What about birds and weather folklore?

When a particular bird's appearance coincided with a regular event, such as geese arriving during a cold spell, this soon passed into the folkloric calendar associated with the seasons. Much of this has survived to the present day, including the belief that the early arrival of wintering waterfowl foretells a harsh winter to come. A nice idea, but don't plan your diary around it!

How else do birds feature in popular culture?

How many ways do you need? Just think of cartoon characters such as Donald Duck and the Roadrunner ("beep beep!"), and hundreds — perhaps thousands — of pop songs featuring birds in their titles or lyrics, from "My Little Chickadee" and "Rockin" Robin" to Vera Lynn's "Bluebirds Over the White Cliffs of Dover" (which were probably meant to be swallows), not to mention the various groups named after birds — the Eagles, to name but one.

PROTECTING AND STUDYING BIRDS

Which was the first bird to be protected by law?

Arguably the sacred ibis. The Ancient Egyptians worshipped many gods, including Thoth, who was often represented as an ibis. Ibises would appear at the time the River Nile rose, and were therefore seen as bringing good fortune, preserving the country from plagues and serpents. Mummified remains of ibises have been found in tombs at Thebes and Memphis. Because of this association with the gods, killing an ibis was considered a terrible crime, punishable by death.

The swarm

The most destructive pest species is undoubtedly the red-billed quelea of the African savannah. The world's most numerous bird, quelea flocks millions strong have been known to strip fields bare of crops, and the destructiveness of these birds has earned them comparison with a plague of locusts.

When was the first bird refuge established?

In 1903, U.S. president Theodore Roosevelt designated Pelican Island, on Florida's east coast, the first U.S. National Wildlife Refuge, primarily to protect nesting waterbirds. In Britain the Royal Society for the Protection of Birds founded its first bird reserve, on Romney Marsh in Kent, in 1930, and that at nearby Dungeness followed soon after in 1932.

When was the National Audubon Society founded, and why?

The original Audubon Society was founded by George Bird Grinnell in 1886, but despite early success its membership soon declined and it was forced to disband just two years later. Then, in 1896, Harriet Lawrence Hemenway founded the Massachusetts Audubon Society "to discourage the buying and wearing, for ornamental purposes, of the feathers of any wild birds." Soon more than 20 other states had joined the cause, and in 1905 the National Audubon Society was founded.

Loadsamoney!

The world's most valuable bird was a racing pigeon called Invincible Spirit, bought by the British company Louella Pigeon World in 1992 for an extraordinary £110,000 (then roughly $170,000). Like an ultravaluable racehorse, it was immediately retired and put out to stud!

Why do we band birds?

Banding (known in Britain as ringing) is the practice of fitting a small metal ring around a bird's leg; the purpose of banding is to learn more about birds' behavior, movements, life-cycles and — especially — migrations. Data from banded birds (either those recovered dead or those retrapped while alive) help us build up a picture of many different aspects of an individual bird's life, and — taken together with data from other recovered birds of the same species — enable us to draw conclusions about

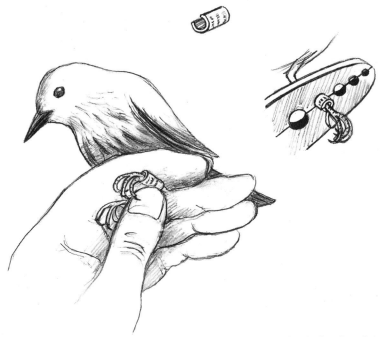

Bird banders collect a range of data before releasing the birds they band. Much can be learned, particularly about bird migration, when a banded bird is recaptured at another location.

the general behavior of the species. Banding can tell us how long birds live, where they spend the winter, how fast they travel when migrating and many other things of great importance to biologists and conservationists.

Does banding harm the bird?

Hardly ever. Very occasionally a captured bird may be so exhausted that it suffers trauma during handling. And, as in any interaction between humans and wild creatures, accidents can happen. But these are extremely rare, and in general banding does no harm to the birds being caught. Certainly the benefits that banding brings to bird conservation far outweigh the risk of harming individual birds. Banders are licensed and to become one takes years of rigorous training.

When did banding begin?

The first person to mark birds using "rings" around their legs was the German ornithologist Johann Leonard Frisch, who in 1740 tied colored threads to the feet of swallows. When the color in the threads did not run, Frisch proved that the birds did not hibernate under water, as had been thought. During the early 19th century John James Audubon tied a silver wire around the leg of an eastern phoebe but did not follow up on his experiment. Then, in 1890, a private landowner in Northumberland in northern England used aluminum rings for the first time, placing them round the legs of young woodcock in order to study their movements.

How did this develop into a formal program?

Early in the 20th century, various ornithologists in both North America and Britain began official programs to band birds. Today, the U.S. Department of the Interior and the Canadian Wildlife Service jointly administer the North American Bird Banding Program, while the British Trust for Ornithology (BTO) runs the British program. Once these organizations have collected enough data, they analyze it in order to learn more about bird movements and migrations, as well as other aspects of their lifecycle such as longevity. The rings used are generally made from aluminum alloy, making them light but strong.

How many birds have been banded in North America and Britain?

To date, approximately 60 million individual birds have been banded in North America, of which about 3 million have been "recovered" (either found dead, or retrapped away from where they were originally banded) — almost 5 percent of the total number of birds. In Britain almost 32 million birds have been banded, of which approximately 600,000 have been recovered (just under 2 percent of the total).

Which species is banded most frequently?

The mallard is way out in front, with an extraordinary six million individuals banded, of which almost a million have been recovered.

What is "color banding" for?

Ornithologists sometimes put brightly colored bands on birds to distinguish between individuals in a particular population so that their behavior can be studied more easily. In the case of larger birds such as gulls or shorebirds, colored dyes are painted onto the bird's plumage so that it is visible from a distance, while large raptors are sometimes marked using plastic wing tags. In recent years larger birds such as eagles, storks and cranes have also been radio tagged using powerful miniature transmitters to send a signal so that the bird can be followed on its migratory journey, giving us invaluable data on their movements and migrations.

What should I do if I find a banded bird?

If you find a banded bird, you should report it as soon as possible to one of the relevant authorities, indicating the band number, color, time and place of discovery. In the United States, either call 1-800-327-BAND or e-mail bandreport@patuxent.usgs.gov. In Canada, e-mail BBO_CWS@ec.gc.ca. To thank you for your efforts, the banding office will usually send you information about the bird, such as what species it is and where it was banded.

What is a bird observatory?

A place where birders and ornithologists go to observe birds — especially during migration. Observatories usually comprise a building and a trapping area, and are commonly situated on a coastal headland or island to maximize the number of migrants and different species likely to show up. Well-known observatories include Cape May in New Jersey, Fair Isle in Britain, Falsterbo in southern Sweden, Long

Point Bird Observatory in Canada and Point Reyes Bird Observatory in California. The very first bird observatory was set up by Heinrich Gatkë on the German island of Heligoland in the mid 19th century.

Which is the most intensively studied bird?

In Britain, the great tit seems to have proved endlessly fascinating. It has been studied in Wytham Wood in Oxfordshire since 1947. In North America, the most-studied bird is probably the Florida scrub jay, studied in Central Florida since the 1950s. Incidentally this bird is the only species entirely restricted to the state of Florida.

What is "ethology"?

Ethology is the study of animal behavior, developed between the First and Second World Wars by a new generation of "observer-scientists," who studied wildlife (notably birds) in the field rather than in the museum or laboratory. Pioneers included the British scientist Sir Julian Huxley, who spent his summer holidays in 1916 watching the breeding behavior of great crested grebes; Niko Tinbergen, a Dutch scientist who concentrated mainly on gull colonies; and Konrad Lorenz, an Austrian who popularized the new science through best-selling books such as *King Solomon's Ring*, published in 1952. At first, their scientific peers looked down on ethologists. But gradually the new science earned respect, culminating in the award of the Nobel Prize for Physiology or Medicine to Lorenz, Tinbergen and Karl von Frisch in 1973.

WATCHING BIRDS

Who was the first birdwatcher?

There are several candidates for this honor, depending on what we mean by "watch." As well as the anonymous cave painters of roughly

18,000 years ago, and Noah, who sent forth a raven and dove from the Ark, there is the scientist and philosopher Aristotle (384–322 BC), who made many accurate (and a few inaccurate!) observations of birds. If we regard birdwatching as being the observation of birds primarily for pleasure, as distinct from study, then one might name the Reverend Gilbert White Vicar of Selborne in Hampshire, England. White lived from 1720 to 1793 and wrote one of the best-known books in the English language, *The Natural History of Selborne*.

What was the first bird book in English?

The first bird book written entirely in English was *The Ornithology of Francis Willughby*, published posthumously in 1678 and edited by Willughby's friend John Ray.

When did the term "birdwatching" first appear in print?

As the title of the book *Bird Watching*, by Edmund Selous, published in 1901.

What is "fieldcraft"?

It is simply an umbrella term for a range of skills and strategies used by experienced naturalists to get closer to birds and other wildlife. It encompasses both knowledge and behavior — from knowing what time of day you are most likely to see a particular species, to avoiding sudden movements when approaching a roosting flock. It includes many tricks of the trade, gained by years of experience in the field.

Who wrote the first field guide?

During the 19th and early 20th centuries, several portable bird books were published in Britain and North America. But the first proper field guide is generally held to be the aptly named *A Field Guide to the Birds*, written and illustrated by Roger Tory Peterson, which covered Eastern birds of North America and was published in 1934. Peterson's technique was simple but effective: his illustrations included arrows indicating "field marks" (the key identification pointers for each species) and depicted each bird in a standardized pose for easy comparison between species. The guide revolutionized birdwatching in North America, selling more than three million copies since publication.

What is "jizz"?

Birdwatchers use this term to refer to a bird's general impression and behavior, rather than any specific feature, which can help identify a bird quickly after a brief glimpse or at a great distance. Jizz is difficult to pin down; it amounts to a combination of the observer's experience with some indefinable but definite quality on the part of the bird — essentially its "character." The origin of the term has been disputed, but it appears to have been coined by the British ornithologist T.A. Coward, who wrote about jizz in 1922.

What is "pishing"?

Pishing is a technique that birders use to attract small birds such as warblers and tits. It can be done in several ways, either by kissing the back of your hand (also called "squeaking") or by making a repeated "pish-pish-pish" sound. Results are not guaranteed, though curiously pishing generally seems to work better in North America than Britain. The noise supposedly provokes the curiosity of small birds, especially those that habitually travel in flocks — perhaps because it resembles an alarm call, which stimulates birds to gather and mob a predator. When it fails, however, pishing can seem pointless and faintly ludicrous.

What is "listing"?

Listing is the keeping of lists of birds seen either over a period of time (e.g., a day, year or life) or in a particular place (e.g., backyard, local patch, state, country, continent or world). Lists can be tailor-made for every occasion. One popular favorite is the New Year's Day list — the original of which British ornithologist H.G. Alexander created on January 1, 1905, when he saw a grand total of 17 species!

What is "twitching"?

Twitching is a British slang term for the dedicated pursuit of individual rare birds, usually those which have been blown off-course and turned up somewhere far from home. It is inextricably linked to listing, since twitching makes the list grow longer. Twitchers are driven by a combination of factors, including one-upmanship, an obsession with lists, the companionship of a tribe or simply the thrill of the chase. They usually do little harm and are often expert at identifying birds — if, in some cases, very little else!

Lady of the list

The longest "world list" is roughly 8,600 species, achieved by the late Phoebe Snetsinger, from Missouri, United States. This represents over 85 percent of the world's total. Having taken up "world listing" at the age of 49 when her incurable cancer was diagnosed, Snetsinger lived for another 20 years before being killed tragically in a road accident while birding in Madagascar in 1999. Her incredible life story is told in her posthumously published autobiography, *Birding on Borrowed Time.*

How many people watch birds?

More than you think! In the United States, the number of regular birders has been estimated at anywhere between 300,000 and 1.3 million, though one survey claimed that there were as many as 46 million — about one in six of the total population. It's almost impossible to define what constitutes a birder, but, judging from the sheer number of bird books alone, few other creatures receive more scrutiny than birds.

Why do we watch birds?

In 1940, ornithologist James Fisher wrote that "the observation of birds may be a superstition, a tradition, an art, a science, a pleasure, a hobby, or a bore; this depends entirely on the nature of the observer." Fifteen years earlier, in 1925, the American writer Donald Culross Peattie had a more poetic view of why we are so obsessed with these wonderful creatures: "Man feels himself an infinity above those creatures who stand, zoologically, only one step below him, but every human being looks up to the birds. They seem to us like emissaries of another world which exists about us and above us, but into which, earth-bound, we cannot penetrate." I can think of no better sentiment with which to end this book

BIBLIOGRAPHY

Boelens, B. and Watkins, M. 2003. *Whose Bird?* Christopher Helm, London.

Bird, D. M. 2004. *The Bird Almanac*. Key Porter Books, Toronto.

Birdlife International. 2000. *Threatened Birds of the World*. Lynx Edicions and Birdlife International, Barcelona and Cambridge.

Brooke, M. and Birkhead, T. 1991. *The Cambridge Encyclopedia of Ornithology*. Cambridge University Press, Cambridge.

Campbell, B. and Lack, E. 1985. *A Dictionary of Birds*. T. & A. D. Poyser, Calton.

Catchpole, C. K. and Slater, P. J. B. 1995. *Bird Song: Biological themes and variations*. Cambridge University Press, Cambridge.

Clements, J. 2000. *Birds of the World: a Checklist–Fifth Edition*. Ibis Publishing, Vista, California / Pica Press, Sussex.

Gibbons, D. W., Reid, J. B. and Chapman, R. A. 1993. *The New Atlas of Breeding Birds in Britain and Ireland*. T. & A. D. Poyser, London.

Goodfellow, P. 1994. *Shakespeare's Birds*. Magna Books, London.

Leahy, C. 2004. *The Birdwatchers Companion to North American Birdlife*. Princeton University Press, Princeton and Oxford.

Lockwood W. B. 1984. *The Oxford Book of British Bird Names*. Oxford University Press, Oxford.

Mearns, B. and Mearns, R. 1998. *Biographies for Birdwatchers*. Academic Press, London.

Richards, A. 1980. *The Birdwatchers A–Z*. David & Charles, Newton Abbot.

Snetsinger, P. 2003. *Birding on Borrowed Time*. American Birding Association, Colorado Springs.

Skutch, A. 1996. *The Minds of Birds*. Texas A&M University Press, College Station.

Todd, F. 1994. *10,001 Titillating Tidbits of Avian Trivia*. Ibis Publishing, Vista, California.

Weaver, P. 1981. *The Birdwatcher's Dictionary*. T. & A. D. Poyser, Calton.

INDEX